Introduction to Behavior: An Evolutionary Perspective

Introduction to Behavior: An Evolutionary Perspective

William M. Baum

Copyright © 2024 by John Wiley & Sons, Inc. All rights reserved.

Published by John Wiley & Sons, Inc., Hoboken, New Jersey.

Published simultaneously in Canada.

No part of this publication may be reproduced, stored in a retrieval system, or transmitted in any form or by any means, electronic, mechanical, photocopying, recording, scanning, or otherwise, except as permitted under Section 107 or 108 of the 1976 United States Copyright Act, without either the prior written permission of the Publisher, or authorization through payment of the appropriate per-copy fee to the Copyright Clearance Center, Inc., 222 Rosewood Drive, Danvers, MA 01923, (978) 750-8400, fax (978) 750-4470, or on the web at www.copyright.com. Requests to the Publisher for permission should be addressed to the Permissions Department, John Wiley & Sons, Inc., 111 River Street, Hoboken, NJ 07030, (201) 748-6011, fax (201) 748-6008, or online at http://www.wiley.com/go/permission.

Trademarks: Wiley and the Wiley logo are trademarks or registered trademarks of John Wiley & Sons, Inc. and/or its affiliates in the United States and other countries and may not be used without written permission. All other trademarks are the property of their respective owners. John Wiley & Sons, Inc. is not associated with any product or vendor mentioned in this book.

Limit of Liability/Disclaimer of Warranty: While the publisher and author have used their best efforts in preparing this book, they make no representations or warranties with respect to the accuracy or completeness of the contents of this book and specifically disclaim any implied warranties of merchantability or fitness for a particular purpose. No warranty may be created or extended by sales representatives or written sales materials. The advice and strategies contained herein may not be suitable for your situation. You should consult with a professional where appropriate. Further, readers should be aware that websites listed in this work may have changed or disappeared between when this work was written and when it is read. Neither the publisher nor authors shall be liable for any loss of profit or any other commercial damages, including but not limited to special, incidental, consequential, or other damages.

For general information on our other products and services or for technical support, please contact our Customer Care Department within the United States at (800) 762-2974, outside the United States at (317) 572-3993 or fax (317) 572-4002.

Wiley also publishes its books in a variety of electronic formats. Some content that appears in print may not be available in electronic formats. For more information about Wiley products, visit our web site at www.wiley.com.

Library of Congress Cataloging-in-Publication Data
Names: Baum, William M., author. | John Wiley & Sons, publisher.
Title: Introduction to behavior : an evolutionary perspective / William M. Baum.
Description: Hoboken, New Jersey : JW-Wiley, [2024] | Includes bibliographical references and index. | Summary: "No adequate understanding of behavior is possible without evolutionary theory. Evolution due to selection is necessary to understand why behavior and organisms exist, how culture evolves, and how behavior of individual organisms develops. Evolutionary theory permits going beyond everyday folk psychology that views actions as done by an agent for reasons known to the agent and done because of the agent's assessment of consequences. Evolutionary theory provides a foundation for a true natural science of behavior, one in which behavioral events are natural events and are understood in relation to other natural events. We no longer see sunrise and sunset as caused by hidden entities or gods, and a scientific approach to behavior should also not ascribe behavioral phenomena to hidden entities like an inner agent or inner thoughts and feelings. This book takes the perspective of evolutionary biology to present the basics of a science of behavior. It begins by discussing what is an organism and then what is behavior. Once we understand that an organism is a process and that activities of the organism are parts of that process, we are in a position to see how behavior interacts with the environment and adapts to environmental covariances and changes in them. The book covers customary topics like choice, stimulus control, foraging, adaptation, verbal behavior, and social behavior, but it does so according to a non-traditional organization consistent with the natural-science and evolutionary framework"-- Provided by publisher.
Identifiers: LCCN 2023023302 (print) | LCCN 2023023303 (ebook) | ISBN 9781394184613 (paperback) | ISBN 9781394184637 (ebook) | ISBN 9781394184620 (epub)
Subjects: LCSH: Human behavior--Evolution. | Human behavior--History. | Behavior evolution.
Classification: LCC BF698.35 .B386 2024 (print) | LCC BF698.35 (ebook) | DDC 155.7--dc23/eng/20230802
LC record available at https://lccn.loc.gov/2023023302
LC ebook record available at https://lccn.loc.gov/2023023303

Cover Images: © kali9/Getty Images, Ed Reschke/Getty Images, Dinodia Photo/Getty Images, Ezra Bailey/Getty Images, Noel Hendrickson/Getty Images
Cover Design: Wiley

Set in 10/12pt WarnockPro by Integra Software Services Pvt. Ltd, Pondicherry, India

SKY10054417_083123

For my dear friend Henry

Contents

Preface *ix*

1 **Organism** *1*

2 **Behavior** *9*

3 **Behavior and Natural Selection** *21*

4 **Covariance** *31*

5 **Measurement** *43*

6 **Stability and Change** *55*

7 **Stimulus** *73*

8 **Choice and Balance** *85*

9 **Verbal Behavior and Rules** *103*

10 **Social Behavior and Culture** *121*

11 **Coda for Instructors** *135*

    Index *141*

Preface

No adequate understanding of behavior is possible without evolutionary theory. Evolution due to selection is necessary to understand why behavior and organisms exist, how culture evolves, and how behavior of individual organisms develops. Evolutionary theory permits going beyond everyday folk psychology that views actions as done by an agent for reasons known to the agent, and done because of the agent's assessment of consequences. Evolutionary theory provides a foundation for a true natural science of behavior, one in which behavioral events are natural events and are understood in relation to other natural events. We no longer see sunrise and sunset as caused by hidden entities or gods, and a scientific approach to behavior should also not ascribe behavioral phenomena to hidden entities like an inner agent or inner thoughts and feelings.

This book takes the perspective of evolutionary biology to present the basics of a science of behavior. It begins by discussing what an organism is, and then what behavior is. Once we understand that an organism is a process and that activities of the organism are parts of that process, we are in a position to see how behavior interacts with the environment and adapts to environmental covariances and changes in them.

The book covers customary topics like choice, stimulus control, foraging, adaptation, verbal behavior, and social behavior, but it does so according to a non-traditional organization consistent with the natural-science and evolutionary framework. It also abandons the concept of "reinforcement," for two reasons. First, the concept of reinforcement derives from the notion that behavior is controlled by its "consequences." This is unsatisfactory because it conjures the folk-psychology idea of an agent evaluating the results of action and because it requires imagining some ghostly cause like "strength" in order to account for the temporal extension of activities. Second, a more adequate and powerful alternative concept exists: induction. Induction explains the phenomena that reinforcement was meant to explain and many phenomena that reinforcement cannot—for example, the problem of the first instance (that action must first occur before it can be reinforced), adjunctive activities, Pavlovian conditioning, avoidance (for which reinforcement theory resorted to fairy tales), and performance on basic schedules of reinforcement. I discuss the problems with reinforcement further in the last chapter, "Coda for Instructors," and those readers who may be familiar with reinforcement theory might want to read that chapter first.

When I was in graduate school, I noticed that textbooks about behavior usually began with a chapter devoted to history and then presented a hodge-podge of topics with no overall connection. I surmised that these travesties resulted from the prescientific state of psychology, from which behavior analysis had sprung. I thought the science of behavior should free itself from the muddle of psychology and present itself as a natural science, part of biology, not as a sub-part of a discipline devoted to understanding mind. I thought I would like someday to write a textbook of behavior, like my undergraduate physics text, that began with basic concepts and then built on those in a coherent framework. This is that book, or at least my attempt at it.

The book is intended for undergraduates and anyone interested in a science of behavior in biology, behavior analysis, and anthropology. It could appeal to students in psychology also. It aims to provide a foundation for thinking about behavior scientifically by offering a conceptual framework with examples from experimental research.

Several people helped me in various ways to produce this book. Carsta Simon, Pete Richerson, Matt Bell, and Dave Ruiz read parts of the drafts, and I owe them many thanks for their feedback. Any mistakes were of my making, not theirs. My son Aaron suggested the title, and my daughter Naomi made the drawings in Chapter 5.

William M. Baum
December, 2022
Walnut Creek, California

1

Organism

We are interested in the behavior of organisms here, particularly animals. Plants may be said to behave, because they exchange carbon dioxide and oxygen with the air and exchange excretions and nutrients with the soil, but this book is about the behavior of more mobile creatures, whether unicellular or highly complex. Before we can understand what behavior is and how it relates to the environment, we must first understand what an organism is and how it relates to its environment.

The biologist H. S. Jennings (1868–1947) studied various protozoa including amoeba. Under the microscope, this single-celled organism looks like a blob that moves by flowing and captures smaller prey like bacteria by engulfing them (Figure 1.1). If the prey moves, amoeba moves with it, overtaking it. Jennings wrote, "Amoeba is a beast of prey, and gives the impression of being controlled by the same elemental impulses as higher beasts of prey."

The first question we face is: What is an organism? Whether we are studying amoeba, rats, pigeons, monkeys, or human beings, what do all of these have in common that makes them organisms? A facile answer would be that they are all living things. That just begs the questions: what is "living"? and what sort of "thing"?

One point is clear: All organisms have a lifespan, come into existence, last for a while, and then die. A non-living thing like a chair also comes into existence, lasts for a while, and then wears

Introduction to Behavior: An Evolutionary Perspective, First Edition.
William M. Baum.
© 2024 John Wiley & Sons, Inc. Published 2024 by John Wiley & Sons, Inc.

2 | Organism

Figure 1.1 Amoeba under high resolution microscope. By SmallRex—Own work, CC BY-SA 4.0, https://commons.wikimedia.org/w/index.php?curid=99796205.

out and disintegrates. So, something more must distinguish living from non-living.

In a word, the something more is *exchange*. While alive, an organism is constantly exchanging matter and energy with its environment. It is constantly taking in energy-rich resources, like food, water, and oxygen, and putting out waste, like carbon dioxide, feces, urine, heat, hair, scales, feathers, and dead cells into its environment. This exchange keeps the organism alive, and when it stops the organism dies.

What is death? We may understand the difference between life and death in light of the laws of thermodynamics. The second law states that in a closed system, entropy can only increase or remain the same, but never decrease. Entropy is the opposite of order or structure. When you put an ice cube in a glass of water, gradually the ice cube melts, loses its structure, and after a while ceases to exist. Its structure has broken down, and that process illustrates increasing entropy. Eventually the water in the glass comes to equal the surrounding air in temperature, reaching equilibrium, and that process too constitutes increasing entropy. Indeed, in the equilibrium state entropy increases no further, and this equilibrium represents maximum entropy.

If we apply the second law of thermodynamics to an organism, we see that death represents maximum entropy, and an organism's constant exchange of energy with its environment functions to keep the organism's state away from maximum entropy. That is to say living consists of constantly taking energy out of the environment in order to keep entropy from increasing and to spare the organism from death. Living means being constantly active.

Being constantly active is not unique to organisms; the only thing constant in the universe is change. At the longest time scale of billions of years, astronomers tell us, the universe is expanding and evolving. At the smallest time scale of tiny fractions of a second, physicists tell us, at the atomic and subatomic levels, basic matter is in constant flux. Show a geologist a rock, and you will hear a story about the processes that produced the rock and how air and water will continue to change it. Show an ecologist a mighty tree, and you will hear how it grew from a seed, developed, and eventually will die, decay, and return to the earth. Everything in the universe is in process. Scientists try to understand the processes.

Like everything else, an organism is a process. What sort of a process? Any progressive change is a process. All motion, for example, like a ball rolling, a river flowing, or a person running. Other processes are changes like growth, development, and deterioration—*any change through time*. Looked at as part of the dynamics of nature, an organism is an ever-active process, taking from the world around and excreting waste into the world around. Being alive means being continuously active.

Consider, for example, the difference between an organism and a machine—say, a car. A car can sit unused and inactive for long periods of time—weeks, or even months—and when turned on begins to run. It has suffered no damage as a result of its inactivity. No organism can do this; as long as it is alive, it must remain constantly active, constantly exchanging with its environment, if it is to remain intact. An organism, unlike a machine, has no off switch. The key difference between a bear and a car is that the bear is constantly active, fending off increasing entropy, even if asleep or hibernating.

Complex processes like a running car or an organism have *parts* that themselves are processes. The car's wheels spinning is a process and part of the car's running. Likewise, an organism, as a process, has parts too that are processes. The human body, like that of a worm, rat, or pigeon, is composed of cells that are themselves living things, processes. A cell also has many parts that are processes, such as metabolism, secretion of hormones and other chemicals, and reproducing. The cell, as process, joins together with other cells to form larger processes, such as organs, and these organs join together to form the organism.

The cells in a body perform a variety of functions and coordinate among themselves to function together. A liver cell performs different functions from a brain cell, a blood cell, or a skin cell. In their diversity, however, is also a unity, because they all work together to form the larger process that we call an organism. The liver regulates sugar, which is essential for the functioning of other cells. The brain cells regulate many other functions, particularly muscle actions. Blood cells transport nutrients, particularly oxygen, to other cells, and some blood cells also remove pathogens and dead cells from the body. The skin regulates body temperature and protects from injury. All the different cells and organs of the body function together in an integrated way, depending on one another, to keep the organism dynamic and alive.

To appreciate this intimate association and cooperation, an example in which it is not permanent is illuminating. *Slime molds* have been studied for a long while, because they form temporary organisms. They exist in two phases. In one phase the cells are separate and function independently, like amoebae. They move through a patch of soil, and each one makes its own way, engulfing bacteria and periodically reproducing by splitting in two. The population increases rapidly, sometimes doubling in a few hours. Eventually the supply of bacteria begins to run out, and then they enter the second phase. Some amoebae begin to secrete a chemical that attracts the others, and those other amoebae also begin secreting the attractant. They all join together to form a slug-like organism that contains anywhere from ten thousand to two million amoebae that all move as one. This slug makes its way to the surface, where it morphs into one or more fruiting bodies consisting of a stalk with a mass of spores at the top. The different cells differentiate and serve different functions. Some make up the stalk, and some make up the reproducing organ at the top of the stalk. The spores disperse by being eaten or by clinging to passing insects and other animals. If eaten, they pass through unaffected, and either method deposits spores some distance away in a new area. Each spore opens into an amoeba-like cell, and the separate phase begins over again.

Permanently multicellular organisms are similarly dynamic, just not in such an obvious way. Like any living thing, a cell comes into being, lasts for a while, and then dies. The cells in your body are constantly dying and being replaced by new cells. You lose hundreds of thousands of dead skin cells every day. In the course of seven years, every cell in your body is replaced (except only your teeth). Different organs are replaced at different rates. Your liver only takes a matter of months to be completely replaced. Your bones are replaced more slowly. So, the organism is not a fixed thing. It is constantly changing: a process.

Adding to the organism's inherent processes is the *microbiome*. Every organism has micro-organisms living in its digestive tract and also on its exterior. Some of these micro-organisms are parasites, but many actually live in harmony with their organism, and many contribute to the welfare of the organism in major ways. Examples abound. Termites would be unable to digest wood without bacteria in their guts that break down the cellulose. Similarly, ungulates like cows depend on bacteria in their stomachs to digest grass and other vegetable matter. The truth is that human beings could not survive without the micro-organisms in our guts and on our skin, because they are both necessary for digestion and to protect the organism from harmful bacteria that would cause infections. For example, bacteria in our gut break down dietary fiber into small molecules that can be absorbed and utilized, and other gut bacteria help synthesize vitamins B and K. Some bacteria in the vagina produce hydrogen peroxide and lactic acid, which suppress harmful bacteria. This mutual interdependence is known as *symbiosis*.

These micro-organisms are so essential to the functioning of the organism that they may properly be considered parts of the organism. So, then just what, exactly, is the organism? All the cells in the body share the same DNA, the same genetic material. The microbiome contains entirely different genetic material. Yet

Organism

all this varied genetic material functions together to keep the organism alive and intact. In all that diversity that all functions together, the body is only a part. Like the body's cells, the microbiome functions in coordination with all the other processes in the body to keep the organism alive and away from maximum entropy, or death.

To appreciate the mutual benefits of symbiosis and its dynamic nature, an example in which the association with the microbiome is temporary may be instructive. The Hawaiian Bobtail Squid has been the object of study for this reason. It lives in the ocean at moderate depth. If a predator should attack, the predator would most likely come from below. The squid remains hidden during the day and comes out at night. It would be outlined against the light of the moon and stars above and easily seen. At night, however, the squid enjoys the companionship of a large colony of bioluminescent bacteria on its underside. An organ on its underside is conducive to holding the bacteria, probably the result of selection for mutual benefit (Figure 1.2). The light from the bacteria serves to confuse predators below, because the squid is less visible against the light above. As dawn

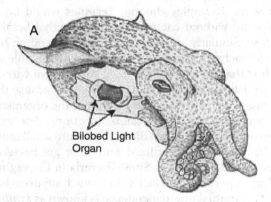

Figure 1.2 Drawing of a Hawaiian Bobtail Squid, showing the organ that houses the luminous bacteria. Reproduced from Jones, B. W., and Nishiguchi, M. K. (2004). Counterillumination in the Hawaiian Bobtail Squid *Euprymna scolopes* Berry (Mollusca: Cephalopoda). *Marine Biology, 144* (6), 1151–1155. Reprinted with permission of Springer Nature.

comes, however, the squid flushes out most of the bacteria, goes dark, and hides. The bacterial colony regrows during the day, and is operational again when night comes.

Now, we may wonder just what is the organism that we call the "Bobtail Squid"? It isn't just the body of the squid, because the bacteria function to keep the squid alive while they have a comfortable home on the squid's underside. They seem to be just as important to survival as many cells that share the squid's DNA. Yet, they come and go in a cyclic fashion, and we are driven to the conclusion that this cycle is also part of the squid as process.

Cycles like the squid's bioluminescent cycle are the rule, however, not the exception. The cycles in a human body are just not so obvious. Every day the bacteria in the gut multiply and are expelled in feces, and then multiply again. The replacement of cells in the body is another such cycle. An organism is an ever-changing dynamic process. In the next chapter we will consider how the organism's behavior is part of that process.

Further Reading

Bonner, J. T. (2009). *The social amoebae: The biology of cellular slime molds*. Princeton University Press. A book-length discussion of research on slime molds.

Jones, B. W., & Nishiguchi, M. K. (2004). Counterillumination in the Hawaiian Bobtail Squid *Euprymna scolopes* Berry (Mollusca: Cephalopoda). *Marine Biology, 144*(6), 1151–1155. A study of the Bobtail Squid's remarkable symbiosis with bioluminescent bacteria.

Nicholson, D. J. (2018). Reconceptualizing the organism: From complex machine to flowing stream. In D. J. Nicholson & J. Dupré (Eds.), *Everything flows: Towards a processual philosophy of biology* (pp. 139–166). Oxford University Press. This chapter lays out the concept of the organism as process.

Nicholson, D. J., & Dupré, J. (2018). *Everything flows: Towards a processual philosophy of biology*. Oxford University Press. This edited volume kicks off a serious exploration of process ontology.

2

Behavior

Organisms behave, but what is behavior exactly? An organism and its behavior are inextricably tied together. There is no such thing as behavior without an organism, and no such thing as an organism without behavior. Behavior serves the organism-process, but how exactly? To understand what behavior is and does, we need to understand why organisms exist in the first place.

We know an organism carries genetic material (DNA) that, together with environmental factors, guides development of the organism from a fertilized egg to an adult form. Why should this be? Why didn't the naked DNA stay in the "primordial soup," the warm water pool rich in amino acids in which it originated?

In fact, the dominant life form on this planet is not so far removed from naked DNA—bacteria. A bacterium is enclosed in a flimsy membrane that lets in nutrients from the surrounding media and lets out chemicals like enzymes manufactured in the bacterium. This membrane is flimsy enough that it also allows fragments of DNA both in and out. Bacteria mutate all the time because transfer of DNA between bacteria goes on all the time. This may be the reason that bacteria are so successful; they are the dominant life form because they adapt to virtually any environment, and they make up by far the majority of the biome of the planet.

So, why do complex organisms exist? Their DNA must benefit somehow. The answer is that the arrangement in which DNA is carried within an organism facilitates the replication of the

Introduction to Behavior: An Evolutionary Perspective, First Edition.
William M. Baum.
© 2024 John Wiley & Sons, Inc. Published 2024 by John Wiley & Sons, Inc.

DNA. The arrangement ensures that copies of DNA in offspring tend to be faithful. This is called *fidelity* of replication. In comparison with bacteria, a multi-celled organism also offers security—the DNA is not so easily damaged. These benefits allowed multi-celled organisms to compete with bacteria and persist in competition with them while evolving immune systems to fend them off—competition that goes on still, as bacteria and viruses invade and challenge the body in what are called "diseases" or "infections."

Biologists often call the organism carrying the genetic material an *interactor*, in contrast with the DNA, which they call a *replicator*. Since interactors exist because of their benefits to their replicators, the interactors function for the sake of copying the replicators. They are selected for that function. In other words, the function of an organism is to produce copies of its replicator—to reproduce. The organism is the way DNA makes more DNA.

That organisms exist to reproduce might seem like an improbable or even uncomfortable conclusion. Indeed, the picture drawn above is simplified, because organisms do not only produce copies of their DNA, they also change the environment in ways that will help their offspring to survive and reproduce. A spectacular example is the beaver dam. Beavers dam up a stream with trees they fell with sharp teeth, creating a pool, in the middle of which they construct a hut that protects them and their offspring from predators and weather. Besides that, the pool encourages nutritious plants to grow around it, providing energy-rich resources.

Human culture may be looked at this way too. The practices of a culture usually create an environment, both social and nonsocial, that is conducive to producing and nurturing offspring. Culture benefits the group in competition with other groups, and the resulting group selection depends on the group's producing surviving offspring. Practices about childbirth and nursing newborns encourage surviving—the maternity ward of a hospital is just an extreme example. We will take up human culture in Chapter 10.

In any population of organisms, only some of the members actually reproduce. Others fail to reproduce because they die or are unable to attract a mate or aren't interested enough. Whatever the reason, the population usually persists, because under most circumstances, the members that do reproduce generate many offspring. That is why the human population on this planet exploded in the 19th and 20th centuries. Now that birth rates have declined to the point where they are lower than death rates, the world's human population will soon begin to decrease.

If reproducing is the ultimate function of an organism, and if processes have parts that also are processes, we need to ask, "What are the process-parts of the organism-process?" Among the processes that keep an organism alive, only some directly affect the environment. For example, the beating heart has no effect on the surrounding world, whereas locomotion changes the locale. The beating heart and circulating blood might be considered part of the physiological processes of the organism, whereas locomotion or eating would be considered behavior. An organism-process counts as behavior if it affects the environment. As we will see, those process-parts of an organism that *interact* with the environment constitute behavior.

For the sake of clarity, let us call these process-parts *activities*. Since every activity is part of the organism-process, the ultimate function of every activity is reproducing. Some activities serve reproducing directly: copulating, nest building, egg laying, giving birth, sheltering and feeding offspring, and repelling predators. They are obviously parts of reproducing. When a rattlesnake approaches the burrow of a ground squirrel, the ground squirrel kicks dirt into the face of the snake, and this sometimes drives off the snake and saves the offspring inside the burrow. The ground squirrel's activity risks its own life for the sake of its offspring.

An indirect but essential part of reproducing is surviving. Generally speaking, an organism must survive to reproduce, although exceptions exist. The ground squirrel risks its own survival, and parents often risk their own survival, because the survival of offspring overshadows the survival of the parent. Praying mantises and some spiders require the male after copulation to be eaten by the female. Research has shown that the good meal enhances the survival of the male's offspring.

Apart from such exceptions, however, reproducing requires surviving. So, surviving is a process-part, an activity-part of reproducing, and any activity that promotes surviving is a part of surviving and usually part of reproducing.

Now we can ask, "What are the activities that function to promote surviving?" Gaining resources is essential; having enough food, water, and adequate shelter are necessary to survival. Maintaining health also is essential—matters like avoiding predators, toxic organisms, falls, and injuries. In social species like humans, relationships with others may be essential, even if that means only coming together to procreate. Solitary confinement is a punishment for humans, and human children raised without social contact ("feral" children) do poorly when brought into society and usually die young.

Figure 2.1 illustrates how these activities all relate back to reproducing (upper right). Each of the three broad processes below surviving has process-parts (activities). Maintaining health for a human has parts like exercise, recreation, sleeping, and seeing the doctor. Maintaining relationships has activity-parts

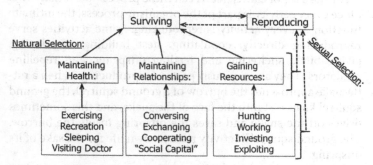

Figure 2.1 *The hierarchy of activities in which each activity is a part of a more extended activity. Note*: All activities ultimately are parts of reproducing. Surviving is usually part of that, and the various activities below surviving are its parts. Each of those activities also has parts that are more specific activities occurring on a smaller time scale. For example, gaining resources has parts like holding a job and hunting. At the right, arrows indicate the possibilities of sexual selection, which operates directly on reproduction by determining which members of a population actually reproduce.

like talking together, exchanging goods, cooperating with one another, and building what is broadly called "connections" or "social capital." Gaining resources includes activities like hunting, holding a job, investing capital and labor, and exploiting resources in the environment.

Every activity, and the various activities shown in Figure 2.1, is part of some wider, more extended activity. Although all activities ultimately are parts of reproducing, they vary in how obvious that relation may be. Hunting or holding a job clearly is part of surviving and, so, reproducing. The function of other activities may be less obviously surviving or reproducing. What about religion? Organized religions establish communities of people who all attend the same church. Such communities often help out in times of financial difficulty or illness, may offer business connections, and may even offer opportunities to find mates for oneself or one's children. What about an artist painting, a musician composing, or a scientist engaging in research; how is the function of that activity related to reproducing? To begin with, these activities sometimes earn a living, but beyond that, these activities often confer prestige and social status, with the result that other people may offer goods and services, even opportunities to reproduce. Some painters find their works selling for large prices, popular musicians have large followings, and successful scientists gain grants and teach at universities.

For the sake of completeness, Figure 2.1 includes at the far right the possibilities of sexual selection, which is selection that results directly by determining who gets to mate. At the top, a dashed arrow leads back to survival, because a female may prefer to mate with a male that will allow her to eat him or will sacrifice himself in other ways for the sake of her offspring. In almost all sexually reproducing species, males compete for access to females, and females choose which male they will mate with. For the female, this choice is usually crucial, because males may not contribute much to the care of offspring and may only be useful, apart from fertilizing eggs, for producing attractive male offspring. A female bird, for example, may prefer a male that has colorful and abundant plumage because its appearance indicates it is healthy. Females with a preference for healthy males would tend to leave more offspring, so such females are selected. If that choice expands across generations, runaway selection leads to phenomena like the peacock's tail. The dashed arrows at the right indicate that in humans, sexual selection may operate at any of the levels shown. A woman may prefer to mate with a man who is healthy, is well-connected, or has abundant resources.

The activities that comprise the three broad activities in Figure 2.1 themselves have parts that are activities. Maintaining health, for example, has parts like exercising, sleeping, recreating, and visiting the doctor. Holding a job includes parts like driving to work, working at a desk or assembly line, talking to colleagues, taking breaks, and so on. Each of those activities has parts. Driving to work entails parts like starting the car, driving on the highway, driving on back roads, and parking. In principle, no matter how specific the activity, it still has component parts.

Figure 2.2 illustrates how activities always have parts and are always part of some more extended activity (except perhaps for reproducing, the most extended activity). It shows hypothetical data—a person's time allocation among activities over some period of time. The chart on the left shows time spent in four activities, labeled "professional activity," "house-holding," "personal activity," and "friends" (socializing). Each of these activities can be broken into its parts. The middle chart shows personal activity broken into parts, like maintaining health, reading, meditating, cooking, and

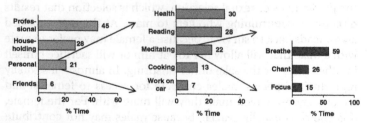

Figure 2.2 *All activities take time and are composed of parts that take time.* Note: **Left**: time allocation among four extended activities. **Middle**: time allocation among the parts of one extended activity, personal activity, including parts, also activities. **Right**: time allocation among the parts of one personal activity, meditating, including breathing, chanting, and focusing. As one moves from left to right, time scale decreases.

working on the car. The chart on the right shows the parts of meditating: breathing, chanting, and focusing.

You may already have noticed that the more extended an activity is, the more time it takes up. Reading a book takes more time than reading a chapter. Loving someone takes more time than kissing someone. Holding a job takes more time than driving to work. As one moves from left to right in Figure 2.2, one moves from broader to more specific activities and from activities that take more time to activities that take less time. A way to talk about this shift is to say these activities exist on different *time scales*, which means that to observe them would require longer timeframes for the ones to the left and shorter timeframes for the ones to the right. As one moves from left to right in Figure 2.2, one moves from longer time scales to shorter time scales.

Figure 2.3 illustrates how activities occur on different time scales. At the bottom, activities like pressing a button take less than a second, and one would record their duration in milliseconds. A pigeon's peck takes less than a second, but still has parts—moving the head forward, closing eyes, opening beak—also measured in milliseconds. The second tier includes activities

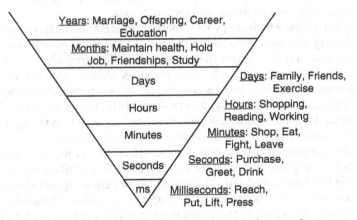

Figure 2.3 *Different activities exist on different time scales.* Note: Some activities take only milliseconds, the bottom tier. As one moves up tier by tier other activities exist, at longer and longer time scales.

that take seconds to occur, like purchasing a box of cereal—placing it on the counter and paying—or a pigeon's flying from a perch to a feeding spot. The third tier includes activities that take minutes, like shopping for a box of cereal, with the parts: entering the store, retrieving the box from a shelf, approaching the cashier, and paying. Though a pigeon's single peck takes less than a second, researchers often take advantage of pigeons' tendency to peck repeatedly by training them to peck at a response key—a translucent key attached to a switch that appears to the pigeon as a circular disk lit from behind. Then the pigeon may be required to operate the switch, say, 50 times before receiving food. This and other more complicated requirements could take minutes. On the next tier are activities that occur on the scale of hours, like a shopping expedition involving multiple stores or playing a game of baseball. Next is the scale of days, which might include activities like working, spending time with family and friends, and exercising multiple times in a week. Beyond days, some activities take months, like attending to health—including visits to doctors and dentists—maintaining relationships with friends, and working. In the top tier are activities that only occur on a scale of years, like marriage—including multiple marriages—holding a job or jobs, and raising offspring. At every time scale, we talk about different activities.

Activities, which are process-parts of an organism's process of staying alive and reproducing, function to maintain the organism because activities affect the environment. Foraging allows capturing food, digging a burrow provides shelter, and defense against a predator improves survival. As we noted earlier, an organism is constantly interacting with its environment. Behavior is the part of that interaction that operates on the environment. Some activities operate on the environment as a result of phylogeny or natural selection. Members of a population that fail to respond to predators or prey leave fewer offspring and tend to be selected out. Those that fail to behave appropriately toward a potential mate ("courtship") likewise leave fewer offspring. As a result, the population consists predominantly of organisms that respond to predators and prey, and that engage in courtship rituals without the need for much experience.

Other activities operate on the environment as a result of ontogeny. Think of farming and pest control in contrast with a hawk's response to a rabbit and a rabbit's response to a hawk. Think of human "dating" in contrast with courtship displays of birds. We will have much to say about both the phylogeny and ontogeny of activities. We will discuss responses to environmental events further when we consider the concept of induction. For now, let us consider the meaning of "interact with the environment."

For an activity to produce an effect in the environment, all the parts of the activity must function together in harmony. A successful tennis serve requires correctly placing the feet, tossing the ball, raising oneself and the racquet, and bringing down the racquet on the ball. For a hawk to catch a rabbit requires positioning, diving, extending the talons, and hitting the rabbit. Holding a job requires getting to work and all the activities that constitute "working."

When an activity changes something in the environment, that change comes back to affect the organism and its activities. The effect coming back is called *feedback*. A familiar example is a heating system, in which temperature is set to a required level (S), called the "setpoint," and a shortfall in temperature (Δ) turns on the furnace (process), producing heat (B), which raises the temperature of the environment (R) and feeds back to reduce the deviation Δ. Figure 2.4 illustrates the basic elements of a feedback system. Some feature of the system sets the requirement S, which determines how the system changes and stabilizes. The boxes indicate processes or activities. Arrows indicate the direction of effects. The organism's activity B is triggered by Δ, a deviation from the requirement (also known as "error"), which is the difference $S-R$, and B is output from the organism. B affects the environment, producing feedback R, which compared with S produces either the same or a new level of Δ.

A simple behavioral example is search. This activity continues until a certain requirement (S) is met, and Δ goes from some level to zero. One may be searching for something specific ("Where are the scissors?") or non-specific ("I'll know it when I see it"), but the activity ends when the thing is found (R equals S) and Δ goes

Behavior

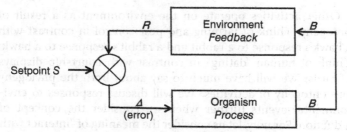

Figure 2.4 *Elements of a basic feedback system applied to behavior.*
Note: Each box represents a process (technically, a transform) with input and output variables. The arrows indicate the way processes are connected by input and output variables. The circle with an X indicates comparison, which results in Δ ("error"), which is input to the organism process. The output from the organism process is input (*B*) to the environment process, affecting the environment and producing an effect represented by *R*. The environmental effect (*R*) compared with the setpoint *S* constitutes Δ.

to zero. A similar example is task completion, like running a race, building a boat, or digging a burrow. The requirement *S* is the endpoint, when the thing being worked on is finished, and when that point is reached, Δ goes to zero. Another example like that is waiting: the setpoint *S* is a particular time, and as that time approaches Δ decreases, and activity may change. Waiting is not passive; it requires checking for the awaited event. Waiting for a friend to show up leads to more and more watching out as the meeting time approaches and Δ decreases. Distance may also work this way: running a race to the finish or a rabbit fleeing to its burrow with a hawk overhead.

These examples all view behavior in a relatively small timeframe. They all describe one-time events. In an expanded timeframe, such events may repeat. A pigeon searching for seeds in the grass spots a seed and eats it, then spots another seed and eats that, and the process goes on as long as it continues finding seeds. In Figure 2.4, *R* represents rate of energy intake from the environment, and *S* is energy intake required to stay alive, a positive number. The difference *S*–*R* equals Δ, and as long as Δ is greater than zero, hunting for seeds persists. In a wider timeframe, task completion also works like this. A runner runs many races, and race-running gains in prestige and money (*R*) as long as Δ remains positive. If S is a maximum attainable recognition, when R equals this maximum, Δ equals zero, and the activity stabilizes. A boat builder similarly builds many boats and gains prestige and money. Waiting also may be seen in an extended timeframe, for example, if we think of predators that lie in wait for prey. Ambush predation means remaining vigilant for prey to arrive and is maintained as long as the rate of prey (R) suffices for surviving and reproducing (i.e., R equals S). Examples include cryptic fish, which wait for smaller fish and swallow them, web-spinning spiders, which wait for flies to get caught in the web, and ant lions, which dig a trap for ants to fall into.

All these examples illustrate what is known as *negative feedback*. This is feedback that tends to correct error Δ, always bringing Δ back toward zero. The process (activity) decreases output B if Δ is negative and increases B if Δ is positive. A governor on an engine, for example, works by changing engine speed in comparison with a set speed S. If engine speed R is higher than S (negative Δ), the governor decreases energy input (fuel), which reduces R. If the engine speed is less than S (positive Δ), the governor increases energy input, which increases R. In the long run, R equals S, and Δ equals zero. Negative feedback leads to stability.

On longer time scales, negative feedback results in balance between behavior and environment, and balance means that R tends to equal S and for Δ to equal zero. In the long run, energy intake meets what is required to stay alive. Staying alive— remaining active—requires energy expenditure, so R represents *net* energy intake: the difference between energy taken in and energy expended. As long as net energy intake suffices for surviving and reproducing, a long-term balance prevails.

Avoiding danger differs from the examples so far, because in the previous examples B increased R, and R was something that promoted survival. When R represents the likelihood of being eaten or injured, activities B act to reduce R rather than increase R. A rabbit flees to its burrow when a hawk appears. Vigilance and running ("avoidance") are activity parts of avoiding hawks. S is a low rate of encounters, and R is risk, actual rate of encounters. Avoidance activity B reduces risk and persists as long as risk R is greater than S; this time as long as Δ is negative. Energy expended in avoidance balances risk, meaning that risk remains at a low enough level to still allow surviving and reproducing.

Positive feedback is the opposite of negative feedback. Instead of decreasing error, positive feedback increases error. For example, if the setpoint fails to constrain R, and R increases B while B increases R. When this occurs, the system runs away, moving to extremes of B, until some other factor intervenes (e.g., the system breaks). You have probably heard positive feedback at an event where a microphone was too close to a speaker, resulting in a loud piercing noise. An example in nature is runaway sexual selection, when females prefer to mate with brightly colored males with elaborate decorative displays. Think of those male traits as B, getting to mate as R. If females always choose the most brightly colored and the most elaborate displays, no setpoint exists to constrain those male traits, and across generations the traits increase to fantastic levels, resulting in phenomena like the peacock's tail. Eventually natural selection caps the sexual selection, because the bright color and cumbersome displays interfere with males' ability to find food and evade predators.

In this chapter, we have focused on the maintenance of behavior. In subsequent chapters we will consider how behavior changes, when we take up topics such as acquisition, extinction, and choice.

Further Reading

Baum, W. M. (2013). What counts as behavior: The molar multiscale view. *The Behavior Analyst*, 36(2), 283–293. This paper explores how to conceive of behavior for scientific study.

Wallace, A. F. C. (1965). Driving to work. In M. E. Spiro (Ed.), *Context and meaning in cultural anthropology* (pp. 277–292). Free Press. This paper describes the parts of the activity "driving to work."

3

Behavior and Natural Selection

If you put a pigeon that has not eaten for a while into a lighted experimental chamber where nothing is happening, the pigeon quiets down and sits still. In the front wall of the chamber is a food hopper, out of which the pigeon has eaten in the past. After a while, you begin delivering small amounts of food to the hopper every now and then. The pigeon eats the food, and its behavior changes dramatically. It becomes highly active, moving around the chamber, flapping its wings, and pecking at things. It pecks at the wall, at the floor, even in the air. Why would this happen?

Pecking is the way an adult pigeon gets its food. A pigeon hatchling in the nest has no feathers—only down—cannot fly, and does not peck. Its parents feed it with crop milk, a fluid that is secreted by the walls of the crop.[1] Eventually, the young pigeon grows feathers and must feed itself. Crucially, it has never pecked at a seed, but its surviving depends on pecking at seeds. At some point, it actually begins finding seeds and pecking at them.

Pecking is an activity native to pigeons. Apart from flying and mating, pecking is the way pigeons get along in the world. Pecking is as much a result of normal pigeon development as growing feathers, flying, and mating. In the situation described

---

1 The crop is a muscular sack in which seeds are ground with small stones and then passed on to the stomach; in a chicken or turkey, it is called the "gizzard".

Introduction to Behavior: An Evolutionary Perspective, First Edition.
William M. Baum.
© 2024 John Wiley & Sons, Inc. Published 2024 by John Wiley & Sons, Inc.

above, the occasional delivery of food approximates the pattern the pigeon encounters when it forages for seeds—a bit of food, some time, another bit of food, and so on. Thus, we say the food *induces* pecking—starts it and keeps it going—whether in the natural environment or in the laboratory. The availability of food greatly increases the likelihood and frequency of pecking.

Why should the food induce pecking? Think of an ancestral population of pigeons. In this population, surviving and reproducing required adequate responses to food, predators, and mates. Suppose that the pigeons varied in the adequacy of their responses. Suppose some were slow to respond to food, obtained less food, were less healthy, and so left fewer offspring. As generations passed, the population would have consisted more and more of pigeons that responded strongly to food. Similarly with responding to predators and mates.

What do food, predators, and mates have in common? Their role as environmental events that affect surviving and reproducing means that they are important in the evolution of the species—in *phylogeny*—and that they will induce activities that acquire food, evade predators, and induce mates to copulate (i.e., "courting") as a result of natural selection across generations. Thus, food, predators, and mates are *Phylogenetically Important Events* (*PIEs*).

The verb *induce* and the noun *induction* are terms that have broad application. Not only pigeons' feeding by pecking but even an amoeba's engulfing a prey may be said to be induced by the prey. They differ in that pigeons are visual hunters, whereas amoeba responds to chemical cues. The phenomena of induction have historically gone by other names, such as "elicitation" and "arousal." A specific event like a seed might be said to elicit a discrete response, a peck, but thinking of temporally extended activities, one would rather say that finding seeds induces pecking. Arousal indicates a vague general state stimulating activities that remain unspecified, whereas induction relates specific environmental features to particular activities. In this book, we will use the vocabulary of induction as *process*, induce as *mechanism*, and *inducer* as the environmental event or phylogenetically important event.

Pigeons in a situation like the one described above not only peck, they become aggressive. If you put another pigeon, restrained, in the chamber, when the experimental pigeon is not pecking or eating, it spends a lot of time attacking the bystander pigeon. If given a mirror, it attacks its own image in the mirror. To understand why food induces aggression when it is removed, one may look at how pigeons typically feed. If one pigeon begins finding seeds, others soon arrive, and the pigeons compete to find seeds. The pigeons keep a bit of distance from one another, and if one pigeon gets too close to another, the other attacks. So, aggression is part of feeding for pigeons.

If you do the same procedure with a rat, occasionally dropping a food pellet into the food hopper, the rat, like the pigeon, becomes highly active. It moves about and chews on anything it can get hold of: a metal bar or a piece of wood. If a water spout is available, it drinks a great deal of water, far beyond any need—this is called *polydipsia*. Typically, a rat drinks after eating, and polydipsia seems to be induced because the food is delivered in bits.

PIEs can be good or bad. A good PIE promotes surviving and reproducing; food and potential mates are examples. A bad PIE threatens surviving and reproducing; injury and predators are examples. Whereas activities induced by good PIEs tend to obtain or enhance the PIE, activities induced by bad PIEs tend to avoid or mitigate the PIE. Research on bad PIEs (also called "aversive stimuli") mainly focuses on avoidance. Some experiments have tried presenting images of predators, but this is technically difficult. Instead, research has focused on mild electric shock, as a proxy for injury. Shocks can be presented through the floor of the experimental chamber and their intensity adjusted to be high enough to induce a reaction but low enough to do no actual injury. If the rat can avoid the shock by jumping over a barrier into another space, the shock induces jumping. If the rat can avoid the shock by operating a lever attached to a switch, the shock induces operating the lever. If a rat receives shocks, it also becomes aggressive and operates the lever by biting it. If another rat is present, it attacks. Shock, as a bad PIE, induces attack and avoidance, thus reducing the threat to surviving and reproducing.

Biologists in the 19th and 20th centuries who studied behavior within an evolutionary framework were called *ethologists*. They observed animals both in natural environments and in the laboratory. They documented a huge number of species-specific activities across a great variety of species. For example, Stickleback fishes received much attention. During the breeding season, a male Stickleback maintains a territory and builds a nest (shaped like a tunnel) in the territory. If another male enters the territory, the male attacks it. If an egg-laden female enters the territory, it swims to her and begins a sort of dance, moving them both toward the nest. If he is successful, the female enters the nest, lays her eggs, and the male enters after her and releases sperm over the eggs. After that, the female swims away, and the male guards the eggs and fans them with fresh (oxygen-rich) water.

Ethologists discovered that the male Stickleback attacked a trespassing male because the males all have a red belly and courted a female because she lacked a red belly and instead had a protruding belly. They called the attacking and courting "fixed action patterns," because their fixity within the species seemed most interesting. They called the red belly and protruding belly "releasers," suggesting a metaphor in which the fixed action patterns would be inside the organism and would be released by the environmental events.

Early in the twentieth century, the physiologist Ivan Petrovich Pavlov (1849–1936) arrived at a similar conception, but in a very different research tradition. Pavlov started by studying stomach secretions in dogs, focusing on how the presence of food (meat powder) in the mouth induced secretion in the stomach. He noticed that the secretions began even before he put food in the dog's mouth, as he was approaching. Like a good scientist, he began to study this phenomenon, calling it "psychic secretion." He soon focused on salivation, because it was easier to study and less invasive for the dog. By interrupting one of the dog's salivary ducts, he could bring the saliva outside the dog with a tube and count the drops.

Pavlov developed clear, replicable procedures consisting of repeated trials. In a trial, he would play a tone for a while and then inject food powder through a tube into the dog's mouth

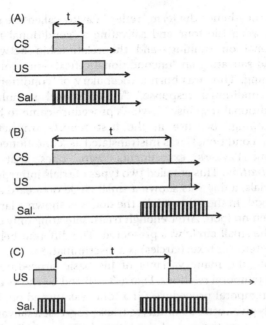

Figure 3.1 *Three of Pavlov's experimental arrangements.*
Note: *CS*=conditional stimulus; *US*=unconditional stimulus; *Sal.* = salivating. **A**: If the duration (*t*) of the CS is just a few seconds, salivating occurs throughout the CS. Researchers call this "simultaneous conditioning." **B**: If *t* is long, salivating begins late in the interval. Researchers call this "delay conditioning." **C**: If *t* is a regular interval from one US to the next, salivating also begins late in the interval. Researchers call this "temporal conditioning."

and record the drops of saliva. After a few such trials, the dogs showed psychic secretion: salivating occurred during the tone as well as after the food (Figure 3.1A).

Pavlov described his research in terms of reflexes, a concept that had been invented earlier to apply to matters like a frog's leg withdrawing when pricked with a pin. The pinprick was called a "stimulus," Latin for "goad," and the leg movement was the "response" to the stimulus. The stimulus was thought to go to the spinal cord and to be reflected from the spinal cord, as in a mirror—hence the term "reflex." Pavlov called the relationship between the tone and salivating a "conditional reflex"—conditional on training—and the relationship between the food and salivating an "unconditional reflex"—not conditional on training. Thus was born a vocabulary of "conditional stimulus," "conditional response," "unconditional stimulus," and "unconditional response." Pavlov's procedure came to be called "conditioning," because in the first reports translated into English, "conditional" was mistranslated as "conditioned."

Among Pavlov's experiments were ones that trained *discrimination*. This entailed two types of trials interspersed. In some trials, a dog was shown a small circle on a card and then given food. In the other trials, the dog was shown a large circle and given no food. After enough trials, salivating only occurred when the small circle was presented. The different behavior in the different contexts (circles) is a discrimination.

Among the many variants of his basic procedure, Pavlov studied temporal relations. Figure 3.1 (B and C) shows diagrams of two temporal procedures. If a tone was turned on, but food was only given after a minute, as trials progressed salivating only occurred near the end of the interval (Figure 3.1B). This was true even if no tone was presented but the food was given at regular intervals, say every 30 minutes. Unconditional salivating followed the unconditional food for a while, but then stopped, and conditional salivating was confined to the last part of the interval (Figure 3.1C). Nowadays, we would call this a temporal discrimination, because no salivating occurs in the early parts of the interval but does occur in the later parts of the interval. Early and late are like the large circle and the small circle. In the experiment with pigeons and food, if the food is presented at regular intervals, the pigeon's pecking moves to the late part of the interval, just before the food will be delivered. That, too, would be a temporal discrimination. Early times induce no pecking, whereas later times do induce pecking.

Researchers after Pavlov found that if dogs were unrestrained and fed by dropping food into a bowl, they exhibited more activities than just salivating: when the signal (tone) came on, they would approach the bowl and wag their tails. Since Pavlov always restrained his dogs in a harness, he had less opportunity to observe any activity other than salivating. We might compare the dogs' activities to the pigeons' activities, particularly pecking as the time of food draws near. As any dog owner will attest, when feeding time arrives, a dog becomes active, salivates, and wags its tail. When pigeons are fed every day at the same time, they too become active as that time approaches, and they start pecking at things.

Different research traditions developed different vocabularies. Reflexologists like Pavlov would use the verb "elicit" to describe their results. They would say that a stimulus elicited a response. This contrasts with the ethologists' usage of "releasing." We can unite all these observations—pigeons, rats, dogs, amoebas, and Sticklebacks—with a single concept: *induction*. As we say the food induced pecking and other activities in the pigeon, we may say that the environmental event (male or female intruder) induced activity in the male Stickleback (attacking or courting). Similarly, we may say of Pavlov's experiments that food in the mouth induced salivating and that a signal of impending food also induces salivating, bowl-approach, and tail-wagging. As noted earlier, even of the simple amoeba we may say that the presence of prey induces approaching and engulfing.

Human beings are by no means exempt from induction. We say a person is "nervous" or "excited" when they are waiting for an event like the arrival of a baby or a lover or an elevator, because we see activities that seem "irrational" or "emotional"—serving no obvious function—like pacing, playing with keys or a bracelet, playing with one's hair, nail-biting. We salivate when sitting down for a meal. People in pain are often aggressive. Worrying never helps, but is hard to control when some significant event is coming up.

The activities we call "irrational" seem to have no function, but they are products of artificial laboratory arrangements or the vicissitudes of modern life. In the organisms' natural environment—that is, the environment in which the species evolved—these activities are induced by PIEs. The pigeons' pecking and attacking, the rats' chewing, drinking, and attacking would all normally be induced by food, competitor, or injury. In the natural environment, these activities all are parts of surviving and reproducing. The same applies to so-called irrational human activities. Salivation functions to prepare for food entering the mouth; it softens food for chewing and begins the process of digestion. Worrying and fidgeting are functional in more natural environments, where worrying may translate to planning and fidgeting to preparation for action.

Our examples so far stressed events that occur regardless of behavior. Food was delivered to the pigeons regardless of the pigeons' activities, regardless of the rats' activities, and a baby or an elevator arrives regardless of the activities of the people waiting for it. In all these instances, the activities induced by the events were responses to the inevitable. They were outside the organism's control, like day and night, to which nearly all organisms respond. Many organisms rest or sleep during the night and are active during the day. Others, like the Hawaiian Bobtail Squid, are nocturnal—only active at night. The change of light to day from night or to night from day induces all sorts of activities, depending on the organism. Crucial activities like hunting or foraging and mating may be induced by the onset of night in nocturnal organisms or the onset of day in diurnal organisms.

You may already have noticed that Pavlov's research introduced another aspect to induction. Food induces salivating, but Pavlov focused on "psychic secretion," the acquired ability of the tone (conditional stimulus) to induce salivating. In the discrimination training, the small circle induced salivating, but the large circle did not. In the pigeon experiment, if a backlit disk is lit for several seconds before delivering food, the pigeon comes to peck at that lit disk—a phenomenon often called "autoshaping." How should we think about these observations?

The tone, the circle, and the light all begin as "neutral"—having no obvious effect—but after enough trials, they become inducers. They induce some of the same activities that the PIE they signal induces. We can call them *conditional* inducers, because they depend on a history of training or experience in which they signal the likelihood of a PIE. Figure 3.2 presents a diagram that gives a general way to think about this training or experience. It shows what is required for an environmental event to become a conditional inducer. When the environmental event (tone, circle, light) is absent, the likelihood of the PIE is low, but when the event is

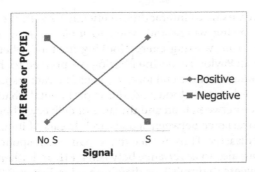

Figure 3.2 *Positive and negative covariance between a signal and a PIE.*
Note: In positive covariance, when the signal is absent the PIE is unlikely, and when the signal is present the PIE is likely. In negative covariance, when the signal is absent the PIE is likely, and when the signal is present the PIE is unlikely.

present, the likelihood of the PIE is high. This is a positive relation, or *positive covariance*, which just means that the likelihood of the PIE varies directly with the presence and absence of the signal. A predator signals the likelihood of injury. A prey item signals the likelihood of food. The opposite would be *negative covariance*, which means the likelihood of the PIE varies inversely with the presence and absence of the signal, and the likelihood of the PIE is high when the signal is absent and low when the signal is present. For example, a signal may covary with safety from a bad PIE (burrow versus predator), or a signal may covary with loss of a good PIE (a predator threatening offspring in the nest). Figure 3.2 diagrams both types of covariance.

The laboratory experiments and the ethologists' observations lead to two conclusions. First, as already noted, environmental events that impact surviving and reproducing (PIEs) induce activities that function in surviving and reproducing by taking in resources, by promoting mating, or by avoiding threats to the integrity of the organism's process. Second, a parallel observation applies to relations between stimuli or signals in covariance with a PIE. Members of a population that responded to such covariance tended to leave more offspring than ones that did not, because responding to covariance in the environment often allows organisms to interact more effectively with the environment. Knowing where and when to look for food saves the organism from wasting energy looking for food when none is available. In Pavlov's experiments, dogs responded to the covariance between the tone and food. Pigeons and rats respond to the covariance between food and the experimental chamber and covariance between food and the time of delivery. They respond also to covariance between signals and threats of injury or loss, avoiding disaster. Thus, we see that organisms respond not only to PIEs but also to covariance between a PIE and other environmental events ("stimuli"), as diagrammed in Figure 3.2. We will examine such relations further in the next chapter.

Further Reading

Breland, K., & Breland, M. (1961). The misbehavior of organisms. *American Psychologist, 16*(11), 681–684. The Brelands, who ran a business training animals for exhibitions, described instances in which food and food-related stimuli induced patterns of behavior that interfered with training. The interfering patterns resulted from natural selection.

Pavlov, I. P. (1960/1927). *Conditioned Reflexes: An Investigation of the Physiological Activity of the Cerebral Cortex*. Dover. This book summarizes a lot of Pavlov's experiments and theories. It was the origin of the mistranslation of "conditional" (the Russian word is an adjective, not a past participle) as "conditioned."

Segal, E. F. (1972). Induction and the provenance of operants. In R. M. Gilbert & J. R. Millenson, (Eds.). *Reinforcement: Behavioral Analyses* (pp. 1–34). Academic. This chapter summarized the evidence supporting induction as a general principle of behavior.

Staddon, J. E. R. (1977). Schedule-induced behavior. In W. K. Honig & J. E. R. Staddon (Eds.), *Handbook of operant behavior* (pp. 125–152). Prentice-Hall. This chapter summarizes a lot of the early research on induced behavior.

Tinbergen, N. (1963). On aims and methods of ethology. *Zeitschrift für Tierpshychologie, 20*(4), 410–433. In this paper, Tinbergen, who was a prominent ethologist, laid out the program of research for ethology.

4

Covariance

1) Recently a 300-pound Black Bear known as "Hank the tank" was in the news. He had been invading kitchens in houses around Lake Tahoe in northern California, harming no one, but feasting on the edibles, bread, breakfast cereal, fruits and vegetables, and so on. In Hank's world, houses were correlated with food, and he went to houses to eat.

2) A park I visited once had a large pond full of ornamental koi. People would feed the fish with food that was available in little packets. One had only to stand on the edge of the pond, and a dozen or more of the colorful fish would rush to the edge in front of you. In their world, person at the edge of the pond was correlated with food, and they went to the edge whenever a person appeared.

3) I used to ask my students if any had a taste aversion. Out of a class of 50–60 students, always several hands went up. For one person the aversion was to bacon, for another canned peaches, for another tequila. After consuming the now-hated item, the student had spent a night over the toilet, puking. Whether the food item had caused the illness or not—the difference between canned peaches and tequila, possibly a 24-hour stomach bug versus overindulgence—the item afterwards would induce disgust or nausea and was shunned. In that person's world, canned peaches or tequila correlated with illness and was avoided.

Introduction to Behavior: An Evolutionary Perspective, First Edition.
William M. Baum.
© 2024 John Wiley & Sons, Inc. Published 2024 by John Wiley & Sons, Inc.

4) In some species of birds and mammals, when mating season comes, the males congregate in a small area; the congregation is called a *lek*. The females arrive, and the males compete with one another to induce the females to copulate. The females are choosy, but eventually each allows a male to copulate. If you are going to mate, the lek is where you must go, both for males and females. The lek correlates with mating and offspring.

5) When I was in high school, growing up in New York City, my male friends and I used to go to Friday-night dances at the Ethical Culture Society. It was an excellent place to meet girls, and for the girls it was an excellent place to meet boys. Both males and females attended frequently, because the Ethical Culture Society correlated with finding a potential mate.

All these examples have two features in common. First, they include a signal or context that functions as a conditional inducer. For the bear, a house (more specifically the back door of a house) induces approach and other food-related activities like salivating. How did a house's back door become an inducer like the tone in Pavlov's experiments (Figure 3.1)? Perhaps a scent coming from a kitchen through a screen door first attracted the bear. A screen door or even an ordinary back door that opens inward is no obstacle to a 300-pound bear. Once inside, the bear followed the scent further, found the food (a *Phylogenetically Important Event*; PIE) and ate.

The second feature all these examples share is an activity that affects the environment in ways that promote surviving and reproducing. Such activities operate on the environment to increase the likelihood of a PIE. For Hank, the house or door constitutes a conditional inducer, but the actual obtaining of the PIE (food) results from Hank's entering the house. The food, in turn, induces eating, which extracts energy from the bear's environment. For the fish, the activity was swimming to the edge of the pond.

Every activity or process functions as part of a more extended activity or process. Ultimately, entering the house or swimming to the pond's edge is part of surviving and reproducing. More specifically, the activity is part of obtaining food. The terms that applied to signals in Chapter 3 apply as well to the relation between entering the house and obtaining food. While the conditional inducer is in covariance with the PIE, so too is the activity of entering in covariance with the PIE. The covariance is positive, because without it, no food occurs, but with it, food occurs.

Figure 4.1 diagrams all the relations involved. The solid arrows indicate induction. The dashed two-headed arrows indicate covariance. The signal (stimulus) and conditional inducer S, which is in covariance with the PIE, induces the effective (also called "operant" or "instrumental") activity B, which also is in covariance with the PIE. As a result of the covariance between B and the PIE, the PIE induces B—that is, the activity B continues into the future (the bear continues approaching and entering houses (B) as long as it finds food, the PIE).

The example with the fish also conforms to this pattern. The conditional inducer S is a person standing at the edge of the pond and is in covariance with food. S probably became a conditional inducer because people stood at the edge of the pond and threw in food. The effective activity of swimming to the edge of the pond in front of the person is in positive covariance with the PIE (food), and the food induces swimming to the edge of the pond whenever a person appears. A difference from the bear example might be that not all people standing by the pond invariably deliver food the way a kitchen invariably contains food. The covariances of S and B with the PIE are positive over time, but result from intermittent occurrences.

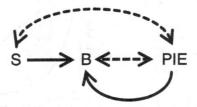

Figure 4.1 *Relations among a signal, an activity, and positive activity-PIE covariance.* *Note*: Dashed two-headed arrows indicate positive covariance between the signal S and the PIE and between the activity B and the PIE. Solid arrows indicate induction. S induces activity B in the short term, and the PIE induces the activity B in the long term.

Covariance

The intermittency of the PIE in the fish example and in most everyday-world examples suggests a slightly different way of thinking about covariance between an activity and a PIE. Figure 4.2A shows positive covariance as a relation between rates: as activity rate or time taken by the activity varies, PIE rate varies with it directly. The solid curve shows a common situation in which PIE rate has an upper limit. This might apply to the fish example, because people only come to the pond at a certain rate, and food cannot be delivered faster than the rate at which people come. The dashed line shows a sort of situation in which the more time is taken by the activity the greater the PIE rate, in direct proportion. This might apply to the bear example, because the more houses Hank visits the more he gets to eat. In positive covariance, the more often the activity occurs the more often the PIE occurs (with or without a limit).

Figure 4.2B shows negative covariance also as a relation between rates. The more the activity occurs, the lower is the PIE rate. The solid curve shows negative covariance with a lower limit, indicating that the PIE generally continues to occur at a low rate regardless. Vigilance reduces the likelihood of encountering a bad PIE (for example, a robber or a predator), but cannot reduce the risk all the way to zero. The dashed line shows the possibility of negative covariance in which the more the activity

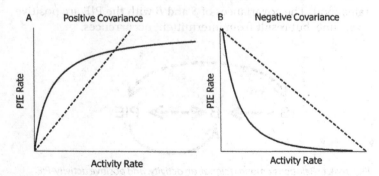

Figure 4.2 *Positive and negative covariance between activity B and PIE rate.*
Note: A: Positive covariance with (solid curve) and without (dashed line) an upper limit to PIE rate. B: Negative covariance with (solid curve) and without (dashed line) a lower limit to PIE rate.

the lower the likelihood of encountering the PIE, without limit. The activity can reduce PIE rate all the way to zero. Such a situation seems unlikely, but examples may exist. For example, the more one behaves in culturally unacceptable ways, the less likely is one to mate.

In the terms of Figure 2.4, the behavior-environment feedback system, the relations shown in Figure 4.2 are feedback functions. They specify how the organism's activities (processes) produce effects in the environment that in turn affect the organism's activities (processes) further. If hunting produces energy intake, in the form of food, and the more hunting the more food, the feedback function would be a straight line like that in Figure 4.2A. If anti-predator activity serves to prevent offspring from being eaten, but cannot always succeed, the feedback function might be like the curve in Figure 4.2B.

The third example above, taste aversion, is notable because it involves a bad PIE, illness. Naming its function, researchers also refer to it as "poison avoidance." In any environment in which they find themselves, organisms will survive better if they sample foods and avoid the ones that cause illness. This is how rats, for example, respond to a novel food—they sample a small amount, and if no illness follows, they consume more. In poison avoidance, the food item (event or stimulus) S is in positive covariance with illness. The effective activity B is avoiding the food item—for example, turning it down when it is on offer or choosing alternatives. The food item S induces the avoidance. However, the effective activity B is in negative covariance with the PIE (illness)—it prevents illness. Figure 4.3 diagrams the relations involved. It resembles Figure 4.1 in all respects except that a diagonal slash indicates that the covariance between B (avoidance) and the PIE is negative.

Taste aversions can be permanent. If someone experiences a life-threatening reaction (anaphylactic shock) to peanuts, avoiding peanuts will be permanent. In contrast, if the illness was due just to accident or overindulgence, the aversion may diminish with time and sampling small amounts. When I was a teenager, I drank far too much cheap red wine at a party, and was sick for a whole day afterwards. For years, I could not look at or smell red wine without feeling queasy. Eventually, after drinking small amounts, I was able to drink it and enjoy it again.

Covariance

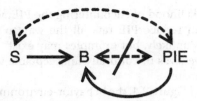

Figure 4.3 *Relations among a signal, an activity, and negative activity-PIE covariance.* Note: The slash through the double-headed arrow indicates negative covariance. S might induce an activity B that avoids a bad PIE or an activity B that misses a good PIE.

In the lek example above (#4), the PIE is mating, and the effective activity B, courting, is in positive covariance with the PIE. The relations shown in Figure 4.1 apply. The lek constitutes the larger context, although one could say that a potential mate (male or female) more specifically constitutes the inducer S, which induces courting. As with a food PIE, mating (PIE) induces entering the lek, both for males and females, across time and mating seasons. This example may differ from the others in that approaching and entering the lek may depend more on selection across generations (phylogeny) than on events within an organism's lifetime (ontogeny). The males and females may gather because those that did so tended to leave more offspring in each generation. Nevertheless, the same relations as in Figure 4.1 appear. Mating (PIE) is in positive covariance with entering the lek, and courting a potential mate, the effective activity B, is in positive covariance with the PIE, which induces and maintains B across time.

The fifth example, human behavior around mating, largely depends on ontogeny, development within a lifetime. The PIE is a potential mate, but the Ethical Culture Society is not the only or the necessary context for courting to occur. The building served a function similar to that served by a lek, but other places could and did serve too. Again, Figure 4.1 applies. The Ethical Culture Society S (conditional inducer), which was in positive covariance with the PIE, induced entering, the effective activity B, which also was in positive covariance with the PIE (potential mate). The PIE, in turn, induced visiting the building repeatedly week after week.

Chapter 2 suggested that behavior constitutes an organism's interactions with the environment. Each activity serves a function that ultimately serves surviving and reproducing. Figure 2.1 illustrated how less extended activities constitute parts that compose more extended activities—reproducing being the most extended. This chapter elaborates on this insight, portraying activities as in covariance with PIEs—more exactly, frequency or rates of PIEs (Figure 4.2)—and thus serving to extract energy and essentials from the environment. Seeing that PIEs may be described as "good" or "bad"—promoting reproducing or threatening it—and seeing that covariance may be positive or negative, we may recognize four different sorts of relations affecting behavior.

Figure 4.4 represents the four types of behavior-PIE relations in a 2 by 2 table. Each cell shows the effect of the covariance on the effective activity B, the activities that the PIE induces, and a common name for this sort of relation. Cell A depicts the

	Covariance: Positive	Covariance: Negative
Good PIE	A Increase/Maintain Induce Activity "Positive Reinforcement"	B Decrease/Maintain Induce Alternatives "Negative Punishment"
Bad PIE	C Decrease/Maintain Induce Alternatives "Positive Punishment"	D Increase/Maintain Induce Activity "Negative Reinforcement"

Figure 4.4 *Four possible relations between a PIE and an activity.*
Note: A: positive selection; positive covariance between an activity and a good PIE. B: negative deselection; negative covariance between an activity and a good PIE. C: positive deselection; positive covariance between an activity and a bad PIE. D: negative selection (avoidance); negative covariance between an activity and a bad PIE. In each cell: (a) the effect on the activity; (b) whether the PIE induces the activity or alternative activities; and (c) a common name for the relation.

situation in which the activity is in positive covariance with a good PIE. Examples are relations like between foraging and feeding or between working and wages. The relation acts to increase the activity if the relation is a recent development or to maintain the activity if it is ongoing. The PIE induces the activity in covariance with it—as courting is in covariance with copulation or attending a church is in covariance with social capital. This sort of relation historically was called "positive reinforcement" on grounds that increase equated to strengthening. A more appropriate term might be "positive selection," connecting to reproductive success or fitness.

Cell C is opposite to Cell A in respect to the PIE. It represents a relation in which the activity is in positive covariance with a bad PIE. These are relations like entering a foraging area and encountering predators or stealing and going to prison. The relation acts to decrease the activity, but may not suppress it entirely, because such relations usually exist side by side with the sort of relations in Cell A. Entering a foraging area also means encountering prey, and stealing also gains resources. This sort of relation historically was called "positive punishment." A more appropriate term might be "positive deselection," connecting to potential loss of reproductive success and selection against the activity. In decreasing the activity, this relation induces alternative activities that are in negative covariance with the bad PIE—that avoid the deselection—like avoiding an area with predators or working instead of stealing.

Cell D (negative covariance between an activity and a bad PIE) is opposite to positive deselection (Cell C) in respect to covariance, but similar in that Cell D represents relations that induce avoidance, except that the activity itself avoids a bad PIE. These are relations like anti-predator activities (freezing, fleeing, or fighting) and avoiding injury or lying to avoid hurting someone's feelings. The relation acts like Cell A to increase or maintain the activity. The bad PIE induces the avoidance activity, because encountering a predator induces anti-predator activity and hurting people's feelings induces lying to avoid that. Historically this sort of relation was called "negative reinforcement." A more appropriate term might be "negative selection," because it means negative covariance with harm, or simply "avoidance."

Cell B is opposite to Cell A in respect to covariance, so it represents relations in which the activity is in negative covariance with a good PIE. In these relations, the activity reduces reproductive potential, as in making noise and alerting prey or lying and losing friends. The relation acts to decrease the activity, but like the relations in Cell C, the relation may raise conflict. For example, lying to avoid hurting someone's feelings may have a side effect of losing a friend. Like positive deselection (Cell C), Cell B represents relations that, in decreasing the activity, induce alternatives to the activity. Instead of rushing, a predator moves slowly to avoid alerting prey. Instead of lying, one sticks to the truth. Historically, the sort of relation in Cell B was called "negative punishment," but a more apt term might be "negative deselection," because the relation means the checked activity is in negative covariance with reproductive potential.

Often the differences between the cells in Figure 4.4 may just be in manner of speaking, for two reasons: (a) loss and gain of reproductive potential may be two sides of the same coin; and (b) alternative activities may be general or specific. Positive covariance with gain (positive selection of an activity) may be the same as negative covariance with loss (negative deselection of alternatives). Do I obey the speed limit to be a good citizen or to avoid fines? Positive covariance between a food and illness might be the same as negative covariance between alternative foods and illness.

More than Cells B, C, and D, Cell A in Figure 4.4 has been the object of much research and clinical intervention. Besides the term "positive reinforcement," this sort of relation induces terms like "incentive," "reward," "self-control," "payoff," "goal," and "nudge." In different fields—popular media, behavior analysis, behavioral ecology, or behavioral economics—positive selection receives all these different labels. But the basic concept is the same: to denote a context and an activity in positive covariance with a PIE that promotes surviving and reproducing. For example, many researchers have been interested in activities called "impulsive" versus activities that are called "self-control." Impulsive activities are ones that appear to be in positive selection in a short timeframe, but are in positive deselection in the long term. Examples include taking heroin, smoking cigarettes, unconsidered purchasing, and gambling. These are all attractive in the short term, but disastrous in the long term. Research has focused on identifying people at risk of impulsivity and inducing long-term advantageous activities.

Common procedures in clinical settings and classrooms include not only positive selection of acceptable behavior (Cell A) but also negative deselection of undesirable behavior (Cell B). A child who completes an assignment may receive praise and a sticker (positive selection) but also may receive time-out for misbehavior (negative deselection). Popular media refer to such combinations as "the carrot and the stick."

Another common arrangement designed to reduce undesirable activities is called "differential reinforcement of alternative activity." In such an arrangement, a PIE (e.g., a toy or video) is offered for a specific desirable activity (positive selection) other than the undesirable activity and is unavailable if the undesirable activity occurs (negative deselection).

Positive deselection occurs in nature. Visiting the wrong feeding area may result in encountering a predator. Eating the green berries may result in illness. Saying the wrong thing may result in a slap. Running a red light may result in a crash. Such covariances are inherent in the environment. In Western societies, however, many people disapprove of positive deselection or "punishment" as a training method or intervention, when it is applied deliberately. Spanking a misbehaving child may suppress the undesirable activity, but may also induce fear and avoidance of the spanking caregiver. A notable exception to the general rule prohibiting positive deselection is the use of electric shock to treat self-injurious behavior in developmentally disabled persons. When someone repeatedly engages in head-banging, positive deselection sometimes seems to be the only intervention that reduces the activity. Clinicians avoid using electric shock, however, because hurting anyone purposely is culturally unacceptable.

The relations in Figure 4.4 provide a helpful framework for looking at behavior in both artificial and natural settings. In the next chapter, we will build on this foundation to see how to measure and study the effects of these relations.

Further Reading

Baum, W. M. (2020). Avoidance, induction, and the illusion of reinforcement. *Journal of the Experimental Analysis of Behavior, 114*(1), 116–141. This paper gives an up-to-date account of laboratory studies of avoidance.

Price, G. R. (1970). Selection and covariance. *Nature, 227*(5257), 520–521. This classic paper introduces covariance as the central principle in selection.

Rachlin, H., & Herrnstein, R. J. (1969). Hedonism revisited: On the negative law of effect. In B. Campbell & R. M. Church (Eds.), *Punishment and aversive behavior* (pp. 83–109). Appleton-Century-Crofts. This paper summarizes research that overcame hesitancy to view "punishment" (positive deselection) as opposite to "reinforcement" (positive selection).

5

Measurement

Anyone who wants to study behavior scientifically needs to address three issues: function, variability, and aggregation. Let us take them up one at a time.

As we have seen, every activity serves a function in the sense that the activity is part of a wider activity. More than that, every activity is defined by its function. Ultimately, all activities are parts of surviving and reproducing, but we usually identify an activity with a more proximate function. Sometimes the name of an activity may imply its function. For example, "shopping" (i.e., for resources), "socializing" (e.g., with friends), or "sheltering" (i.e., from illness or injury). Whatever the activity, however, part of its identity must be its function. For example, "walking" may be a process, but it fails to specify a particular activity, because it could be part of any number of activities. As the name of an activity, "walking" falls short, because it says nothing about function. It tells us nothing about how it fits into a wider pattern of behavior. In contrast, "walking to the store" specifies an activity, because it points toward function; this activity is part of "going to the store" or perhaps "shopping." It might be part of going to the store to get bread. Like any activity, walking to the store has parts, like crossing Sutter Street and walking to Powell Street. Going to the store might have other parts than walking to the store, like bicycling to the store, just as driving to work might have parts like taking the highway or taking back roads. The function of any activity is the wider activity in which it plays a part.

Introduction to Behavior: An Evolutionary Perspective, First Edition.
William M. Baum.
© 2024 John Wiley & Sons, Inc. Published 2024 by John Wiley & Sons, Inc.

The way an activity looks to an observer cannot suffice to specify the activity. If I see a person sitting and holding an open book, I cannot say what activity is occurring. It might be reading for entertainment, reading for information, searching, or pretending. I can only discover the function—and identify the activity—by observing in a larger timeframe: whether for example, the person praises the writing, explains a concept, quotes a phrase, or, in contrast, puts the book away as soon as I leave. Similarly, if we observe a rat in an experiment pressing a lever, we must observe in a wider timeframe to determine if the rat is gaining food or avoiding electric shock. To identify the activity, one must identify the function.

The need to identify function becomes crucial when we observe behavior that appears to be dysfunctional. A male Bower Bird that builds an elaborate bower may seem to be expending a great deal of effort for an obscure function. The bower might seem dysfunctional until we see a female arrive to inspect it and perhaps mate with him. When a person engages in activities that appear to go against the person's surviving and reproducing, therapists look for the function within the dysfunction. If the person refuses to leave the house, the function of staying in may be to avoid some situation that the person finds threatening, like looking for a job. Much apparently dysfunctional behavior turns out to be avoidance, but if the avoidance is successful, the situation being avoided may be difficult to spot. When a child misbehaves in a classroom—yelling, hitting other children, running around—the child's activity may function to avoid assignments, gain attention, or escape into time-out. A practitioner in this situation may conduct a "functional analysis," in which the activity is observed under different conditions, presenting different possible inducers—attention, avoidance, or playing with toys—trying to identify the activity as, for example, gaining attention or avoiding class work.

Figure 5.1 shows the results of a functional analysis of problem behavior in a five-year-old boy diagnosed with autism. The researchers aimed to identify the function of the problem behavior, which they defined as "hitting, kicking, throwing things, self-injury, and screaming." They suspected that these

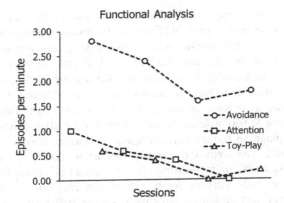

Figure 5.1 *Results of functional analysis of problem behavior in a five-year-old boy.* Note: When problem behavior avoided working on an assigned task, problem behavior increased, whereas when problem behavior brought attention or a preferred toy, problem behavior remained rare. The difference indicates that the function of the problem behavior was avoidance of required work. Data from Kronfli et al. (2021).

activities had the same function—in present terms, that they all were parts of a wider activity. They tried correlating different inducers with the problem behavior to see which ones would induce it. In different 10-minute sessions, when problem behavior occurred, the researcher either briefly paid attention, allowed avoidance of a task (solving a puzzle), or offered a toy that the child preferred to play with. An observer pressed a button every time some problem behavior occurred. The vertical axis in Figure 5.1 shows how often the observer pressed the button. In the sessions where problem behavior avoided a directed task, problem behavior increased in frequency (the observer pressed the button more often), whereas attending and offering a toy had no effect. Thus, the function of the problem behavior was avoiding requested tasks.

Once we know the activity's function, we have identified it. Next will come research activities that aim to understand the activity further and perhaps reduce or increase it. (Research activities also serve functions, such as improving education, helping parents, obtaining a job, or publishing a report.)

A universal property of all activities is *variability*. An activity varies in several ways: in its form, in its duration, and in its rate. Any of these may be the focus of research or intervention. The form of the activity may be irrelevant if, say, we regard lever pressing as feeding or walking as maintaining health, and we aim to understand how to sustain the activity. Whether I walk to the store or drive may not matter if my concern is too much shopping or too little shopping. Form could matter, however, in a campaign to reduce drivers' speed or induce people's use of seat belts. The form of the activity becomes crucial when one is training a skill or facilitating effective social behavior. In ballet practice, only correct form serves the function of gaining approval and applause. Kicking a soccer ball past the goalie requires correct balance and placement of feet. When someone offends others with inappropriate utterances, only forming utterances correctly will enable promoting good relationships.

Activities vary in *duration* because activities are episodic. A common pattern to a day might be working, exercising, socializing, caring for spouse and offspring, and sleeping. On different days, these activities may or not occur, and if they do occur, they may take up different amounts of time. One day, I might work overtime, and another day, I might take off early. I may exercise for an hour, or just 30 minutes. This variability in duration may interest me if driving to work on the highway takes less time, but driving to work on back roads is more relaxing. Variability in duration could become an issue for research or intervention if time spent caring for spouse and offspring varies so much that I seem unreliable, if family never know whether I will show up. In contrast, too little variability might make one seem dull or obsessive.

Figure 5.2 illustrates with hypothetical data how episodic activities may be measured. At the top, the time lines of four activities appear for four consecutive days. When the line is elevated, an episode of the activity occurred. The four activities are gaining resources, socializing, maintaining health, and spending time with spouse and offspring. Gaining resources might be working; it occurs in uninterrupted episodes on Day 1 and Day 4 and with brief interruptions for maintaining health (e.g., exercising) on Day 2 and socializing on Day 3. Most

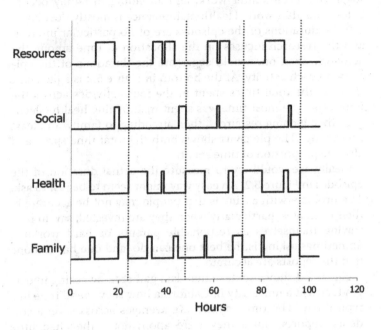

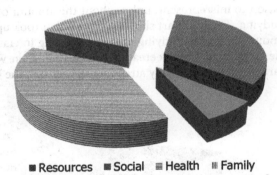

Figure 5.2 *Episodes of activities and their aggregation. Note:* Top: Hypothetical episodes of four activities over four days. Bottom: Pie chart showing aggregation of the episodes of the four activities by adding up the time they took.

socializing occurs after work, and attending to family occurs before and after work. Health maintenance is mostly sleeping.

If the durations of the episodes are of no particular interest, and the research focuses on the allocation of time among the activities, then one would aggregate the durations of the episodes of each activity. At the bottom in Figure 5.2 is a pie chart showing the total times spent in the four activities across the four days. The most time was spent maintaining health (sleeping), then gaining resources, then attending to family, and least socializing. The pie chart shows both the total time spent and also the proportion of time spent.

Ideally, we would try to measure the actual duration of the episodes in Figure 5.2. An easy way might seem to be just to ask. The problem with asking is that people may not be accurate in their estimates, particularly when they are invested, say, in portraying themselves as responsible parents or hard working. Sometimes asking is the best one can do, and one has to hope that the reports are accurate.

Figure 5.3 shows some actual data gathered by asking undergraduates at a university in California how they spend time in a typical day. The times shown are averages across several students' reports. Since they were anonymous, they had little reason to misrepresent, unless about the amount of time spent studying. The pie chart shows activities that took up significant amounts of time. Studying and participating in classes took up the most time, then recreation and eating, then working at a part-time job, and finally attending to health in the bathroom.

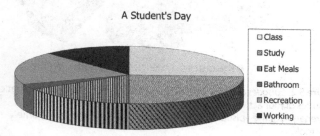

Figure 5.3 *Time allocation in a student's typical day.* Note: Times are averages of several students' estimates.

Figure 5.4 is adapted from data gathered by the United States Bureau of Labor Statistics on about 10,000 households in the year 2015. Participants kept diaries in which they recorded their activities. The figure shows the proportion of time taken by various activities. The greatest share was taken by maintaining health, because that activity includes sleeping as a part, and sleeping typically takes about a third of the 24 hours in a day. Second is gaining resources, then reproductive activities, including attending to family and spouse, and a small proportion taken by socializing. One small sliver shows time taken in activities that did not seem to fit anywhere.

Figure 5.4 also includes a reminder that every activity is composed of parts that are also activities. Gaining resources is broken apart at the right into its constituent parts: working, eating, buying things, and educational activities, in the order in which they take time.

A more accurate way to gather such data on time taken is to observe and record, but such observation is tedious and labor-intensive. Still, as we see in Figure 5.1, researchers sometimes must resort to observation. Pressing a button simplifies the observer's task, but the measure of the activity becomes number or rate

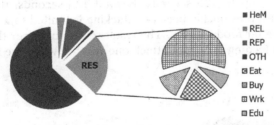

Figure 5.4 *Time allocation in the USA from the Bureau of Labor Statistics.* Note: Left: maintaining health (HeM) took up the largest amount of time, then gaining resources (RES), then reproductive activities (REP; e.g., family and children), then relationships (REL; e.g., friends). The narrow black slice (OTH) represents time taken by activities that researchers were unable to classify. Right: gaining resources broken out into its component parts. Working (Wrk) took up the most time, then eating (Eat), then buying things (Buy; e.g., shopping), then educational activities (Edu).

of the observer's button pressing. This measure could stand in for time because the episodes of problem behavior were always relatively brief and relatively uniform. Each button press represented approximately the same amount of time spent in problem behavior, so the number of presses was a good indicator of time.

Figure 5.5 shows a similar measurement challenge to the functional analysis in Figure 5.1. The pie charts indicate the sort of change in time allocation that we would see in an experiment on food-induced attacking in a pigeon. A subject pigeon was fed bits of food at regular intervals in an experimental chamber where another pigeon was present. The bystander pigeon was contained in transparent plastic box that prevented any actual harm. When the food was delivered frequently—every 15 seconds—we see an allocation like that on the left (Time 1), with most time taken by resting and feeding, a small amount of time attempting to court the bystander, and a small amount of time attacking the bystander. If one delivers the food less often—every 60 seconds—the allocation shifts to include more attacking than any other activity, as shown in the pie chart on the right. The problem is: how do we document this effect to be able to report it for others to see?

Figure 5.6 depicts a similar approach as in Figure 5.1 to measuring time taken attacking the bystander pigeon. The graph shows the rate of attack as the interval between food deliveries varied. The rate of attack increases as the inter-food interval increases, up to 120 seconds. Beyond 120 seconds, the rate decreases, presumably because attacking is limited to a period of time after food is eaten. The result seems to mirror the way pigeons feeding in a flock attack one another when the food is

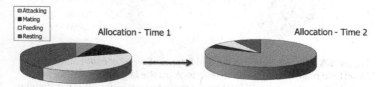

Figure 5.5 *Food-induced attack in a pigeon as time allocation. Note*: Left (Time 1): Allocation when food is absent altogether. Right (Time 2): time allocation when small amounts of food are delivered periodically. Time taken by attacking a bystander pigeon increases greatly, and decreases time taken by other activities.

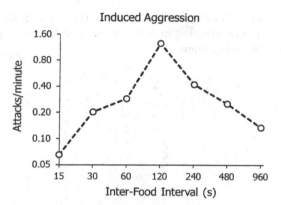

Figure 5.6 *Results from one pigeon in an experiment on food-induced aggression. Note*: As the interval between food deliveries increased, rate of attacking the bystander pigeon increased up to 120 s and then decreased for longer intervals. Data from Flory (1969).

running out. As with the button pressing in Figure 5.1, the estimate of time attacking derives from switch operations, but with an important difference. Instead of the button, the researcher attached the box containing the bystander pigeon to a switch that operated when the subject pigeon attacked with sufficient force to move the box. This automated the recording, eliminating the need to have an observer pressing a button.

As you might imagine, automating measurement is attractive. It has at least two advantages: (a) it saves labor, speeding the research; and (b) it eliminates the need for the observer to make judgments about misbehavior or attacking that might be inaccurate. Whatever the mode of attack, whether pecking or hitting with a wing, it was recorded by the operation of the switch if it was vigorous enough. The activities' function was attacking. Whenever possible, researchers arrange for the activities under study to operate micro-switches, rather than estimate time taken directly. This seems to work well as long as each operation of the switch corresponds to roughly the same amount of time taken.

As we will see in subsequent chapters, using operations of a switch to measure time taken by an activity is common in laboratory research. Pigeons operate keys attached to switches by pushing or pecking them (Figure 5.7). Rats operate levers by pushing, biting, licking, and pawing them (Figure 5.8). Monkeys operate levers by pressing or biting them, and humans operate buttons by pressing them.

Figure 5.7 *A pigeon in a typical experimental chamber. Note*: pecking may occur at either of the three keys, and food is accessible through the square hole below the keys when the grain hopper is raised. A box behind each key contains lights that can transilluminate the translucent keys with various colors. Drawing by Naomi L. Baum.

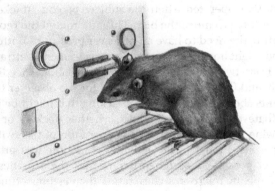

Figure 5.8 A rat in a typical experimental chamber. *Note*: The rat presses the lever, and occasionally a pellet is dropped into the food hopper on the left. Two lights may be lit or unlit to provide stimuli. The floor of the chamber consists of bars, allowing mild electric shocks to be delivered to the rat's feet. Drawing by Naomi L. Baum.

Further Reading

Flory, R. K. (1969). Attack behavior as a function of minimum inter-food interval. *Journal of the Experimental Analysis of Behavior, 12*(5), 825–828. The data in Figure 5.6 came from this experiment.

Kronfli, F. R., Lloveras, L. A., & Vollmer, T. R. (2021). Applications of the matching law to observe shifts in problem behavior: A proof-of-concept study. *Behavioral Interventions*, 1–14. DOI: 10.1002/bin.1810. The data in Figure 5.1 came from this study.

6

Stability and Change

Sometimes life seems to fall into routines. Each day or week seems little different from the one before it. Say, I have a steady job that I go to Monday through Friday, and that the weekend is filled with errands and recreation with family and friends. This stable set of activities could continue indefinitely. Sooner or later, though, something changes. I have a child or change my job or get married or divorced. Then a period of adjustment begins, until life again stabilizes.

Adjustment to change, more generally called "adaptation," constitutes a major development in species' evolution. The ability to adapt within an organism's lifetime provides a boost to reproductive success. Those individuals within a population that were able to adapt to changes in food availability or weather patterns would have left more surviving offspring. Hence, ability to adapt is selected, and populations today possess this flexibility.

The ability to adapt to changing environment is known as *phenotypic plasticity*. Behavioral adaptation represents only one type of phenotypic plasticity. Fish respond to the presence of predatory species with changes in coloration and body shape. Caterpillars that feed on Oak trees resemble Oak flowers in early summer and resemble twigs in late summer. Sex in many turtle species is determined by the temperature at which eggs incubate: lower temperature produces males; higher temperature produces females. When we turn to behavior, the possibilities of

Introduction to Behavior: An Evolutionary Perspective, First Edition.
William M. Baum.
© 2024 John Wiley & Sons, Inc. Published 2024 by John Wiley & Sons, Inc.

behavioral flexibility, of change followed by stability, are greatly multiplied.

Researchers study changing behavior and stable behavior both in the field and in the laboratory. Change involves one of three types: (a) shift in time allocation among established activities, as for example, if one's job requires more effort; (b) introduction of some new activity, as for example, getting married; or (c) cessation of an old activity, as for example, getting divorced. Each of these changes is followed by stabilization of the mix of activities, in the allocation of time among one's regular activities. Change due to introducing a new activity is *acquisition*. Change due to ceasing an old activity is *extinction*.

In the rapidly changing cultures of the world today, examples of acquisition abound. Think of the advent of cellphones and smartphones and concern over climate change. Changes are occurring in the behavior of wildlife. We saw examples of this in Chapter 4, with Hank the bear's house invasions and the approach of fish to the person by the pond. In those examples, we inferred some sort of acquisition event. A documented example of acquisition that was recently in the news was recorded with the help of a field camera tripped by motion. Researchers located the nest of a large female Burmese python in Florida, where these invasive snakes have become a threat to indigenous wildlife. The snake had laid about 30 eggs, guarded them some of the time, but left them unguarded sometimes. A Bobcat came and began eating the eggs. The researchers hailed this observation as good news, because the snake population has been exploding in the absence of predators. The Bobcat's activity has to represent acquisition because the snakes are recent arrivals in Florida, not native, whereas the Bobcat is native.

Acquisition of a simple activity like pressing a button may be abrupt, complete the first time. Acquisition of a complex skill may be gradual. Kicking a soccer ball, sewing quilts, or milking a goat all require acquisition of several parts—placing the feet, swinging the leg, threading the needle, putting together the pieces, stitching, getting the goat on a platform, washing the udders, carefully squeezing the teat. Skill requires practice.

Acquisition often relies on induction. Skills are usually instructed. A player is shown how to place the foot when kicking a goal in soccer. The verbal instructions and modeling induce imitation of similar behavior. The same holds for quilting and for milking a goat.

A laboratory example of acquisition by induction is *autoshaping*. A pigeon in an experimental chamber is fed small amounts occasionally. As we saw earlier, the food induces several activities, including pecking at various things. Training the pigeon to peck a key requires only directing the pecking at the key. If the key is mostly unlit, but lit for several seconds prior to presenting food, pigeons soon come to peck at the key. To close a loop, one arranges that pecks produce the food. Then the food induces pecking the key, pecking the key produces the food, the food induces pecking, and so on. Figure 6.1 illustrates the process of acquisition.

On the left in Figure 6.1, the diagram shows the environment (E) providing a PIE (food), which induces activities in the organism (O). The activity that will be acquired is labeled B (pecking at the key), whereas other activities induced are labeled B_O. On the right in Figure 6.1, the upper arrow ("covariance") indicates that pecking the key (B) is now in covariance with the food, because it produces the food, closing the loop. The PIE induces B and also depends on B. Notably, the PIE continues to induce other PIE-related activities (B_0) that may compete with B.

The speed of acquisition as illustrated in Figure 6.1 depends on the tightness or looseness of the covariance. If you place a rat in an experimental chamber with a food hopper and a lever, and you deliver food pellets occasionally to the food hopper, eventually the rat eats the pellet every time it drops. If then you require an operation of the lever to produce the pellet, instead of delivering them

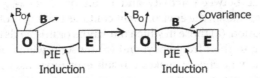

Figure 6.1 *Covariance closes a loop to maintain effective (operant) activity.*
Note: **Left**: a PIE (e.g., food or shock) from the environment (E) induces various activities (B and B_O) in the organism process (O). **Right**: covariance imposed between B and the PIE results in a loop, in which the activity B produces the PIE and the PIE induces the activity, which again produces the PIE, and so on.

freely, after a while the rat, in its movements around the chamber, operates the lever. If the lever is right next to the food hopper, almost at once the lever operates again. Covariance between lever operating and food is extremely tight, and acquisition is extremely rapid. In contrast, suppose operation of the lever only produces the pellet after several seconds' delay, or suppose that pellets continue to drop freely at the same time as lever operations will also produce them. The covariance between lever operating and food is looser, and acquisition is slower.

Looseness of activity-PIE covariance affects both acquisition and also maintenance of the activity. The looser the covariance, the lower the activity rate. Moreover, covariance is never perfect. The feedback functions shown in Figure 4.2 are idealizations. When the relations are actually measured, always variation occurs around the curve or line. Figure 6.2 shows two examples from an experiment with rats, as in Figure 5.8. The top graph shows the feedback function for a relation that puts an upper limit on rate of pellet delivery, and the bottom graph shows a linear feedback function. The data were generated by dividing several sessions into consecutive sampling intervals: 120 s in the top graph and 10 s in the bottom graph. All the samples with the same number of operations of the lever ("presses") were aggregated, and the pellet rate for each of these press rates was also calculated. Each data point shows the pellet rate for one press rate. The square in each graph shows the mean of the data. For each relation, covariance is less than perfect, because the points gather around the curve or line but do not lie on it.

Much research has explored the variety of relations that create covariance between activity and result or effect (e.g., a PIE). Broadly speaking, the environment contains two types of activity-effect relation: (a) those in which our labors or misdeeds bear fruit according to their frequency; and (b) those in which passage of time, as ally or enemy, makes a result ever more likely. We may think of the first as producing or working, because the more of the activity, the more the results. A farm laborer paid by the bushel of fruit picked receives wages according to a work relation. The second type includes all waiting games, in which one must wait and occasionally check whether the result is available. Waiting for an important email message requires occasional checking, but the

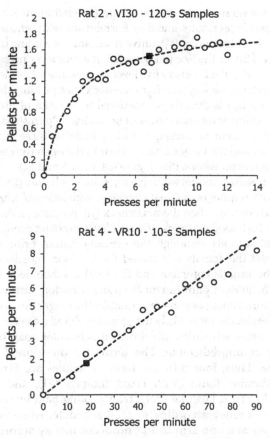

Figure 6.2 *Feedback functions extracted from data. Note:* **Top:** A feedback function with an upper limit to PIE rate, for a VI schedule. **Bottom:** A linear feedback function for a VR schedule. Squares indicate means.

check cannot bring the delivery closer, even though the rate of checking determines how soon one gets the email after it has been delivered. In practice, the two types of relation may combine in some way that both work and time affect the likelihood or rate of result. For example, hourly wages are paid according to time working, but employers expect some amount of work as well. In the laboratory, the two types may be studied separately.

Experimenters model the first type of relation, in which only activity produces results, and time is irrelevant, with *ratio schedules*. Such a schedule maintains positive covariance according to the line in Figure 4.2A or the line in Figure 6.2. If a rat's lever pressing produces a food pellet for every five lever presses, the schedule pays off in much the same way as a farm laborer's fruit picking; the rate of food or money is directly proportional to the rate of pressing or picking. Unfavorable outcomes of an activity ("punishers" or bad PIEs) often occur according to ratio schedules; three strikes and you're out, and the longer a rabbit feeds in the open the more likely it encounters predators. (See Figure 4.4, cells A and C.)

Experimenters model waiting games, in which only time matters and which require occasional checking, with *interval schedules*. A timer determines when the next check will produce an outcome—good or bad, food or shock. If a rat's lever pressing produces food every 30 seconds, although the pressing cannot bring the food closer, still the activity is required for the food actually to occur when the time is complete and the food is scheduled. Although ratio schedules of punishment are more common, interval schedules of punishment occur—for example, the longer one waits to go to the dentist the more likely the dentist will find a cavity.

Both ratio schedules and interval schedules may be either regular or unpredictable. The terms for these are *fixed* and *variable*. Thus, four different basic schedules are Fixed Ratio (FR), Variable Ratio (VR), Fixed Interval (FI), and Variable Interval (VI). A farm laborer's fruit picking paid by the bushel produces money according to a FR schedule, whereas a gambler's play at a one-arm bandit produces money according to a VR schedule. For either, the more of the activity, the more the rate of payoff, but the gambler's payoffs are unpredictable, whereas the laborer's payoffs are regular and predictable. VR schedules typically specify a certain probability of outcome for an action (press or peck). In a FI schedule, a certain fixed amount of time must pass before action produces an outcome. It models the situation in which a train or a friend is due to arrive at a certain time; checking early is useless, but as the time approaches checking occurs increasingly often. In a VI schedule, the amount of time that must pass is variable from occasion to occasion; the outcome is unpredictable but one must keep checking for it.

Much research has focused on these four types of schedule with good PIEs—most often food, but with humans, money—as the outcome. Ratio schedules generate high rates of activity, because the higher the activity rate, the higher the PIE rate. A rat, pigeon, monkey, or human exposed to a FR schedule pauses a while and then completes the ratio at a high rate, resembling situations of task completion like writing a term paper, filling out a form, or building a wall. As the ratio requirement becomes larger, the pause before executing the ratio (task) increases, until eventually, when the ratio is too high, it crosses a threshold, and activity ceases. VR schedules also generate extremely high activity rates, except that any pauses are short and irregular. The bottom graph in Figure 6.2 shows performance on a VR 10 with lever-operating rates ranging up to 90 per minute. In casinos or Pachinko parlors, the rates of play at VR-like machines can be astonishingly high. If the payoff probability becomes too low, activity ceases, when you "can't win for trying."

Figure 6.3 illustrates these properties of ratio schedules. The lines show feedback functions for four different ratio schedules. The slope of a line specifies the ratio of payoff rate to activity rate—the reason these are called "ratio" schedules. As the ratio

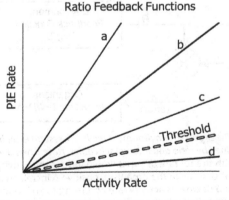

Figure 6.3 *Ratio schedule feedback functions are lines. Note:* The lower the slope, the leaner the schedule. Lines *a, b,* and *c* maintain the activity, but a threshold exists. As the line approaches the threshold, ratio "strain" occurs—i.e., more pausing occurs—and line *d*, which falls below threshold, does not maintain the activity at all.

increases, the schedule becomes leaner, and the slope of the line decreases, from line *a* to *b* to *c*. The schedules that specify these lines all generate high activity rates, with pauses in FR and largely without pauses in VR. When the slope of the feedback line falls below the (dashed) threshold line, activity ceases. Line *d* does not maintain activity.

The concept of a behavior-environment feedback system helps to understand the properties of ratio schedules. Figure 6.4 shows a feedback system like that in Figure 2.4. The organism's process of induction increases or decreases activity rate B, depending on whether Δ is positive or negative. The environment includes a feedback function (upper box) that produces a payoff rate R according to a relation expressed by the notation $R=g(B)$. That payoff rate R is compared with a payoff rate R^*, the payoff rate that would induce rate B without the schedule covariance (as in Figure 6.1 on the left) expressed as $R^* \rightarrow B$; Δ equals $R-R^*$. If the actual payoff rate R exceeds R^*, Δ is positive, and B increases (lower box) according to the relation $B=f(R+\Delta)$. For example, suppose B equals a relatively low rate of 20 pecks per minute, and the schedule is VR 10. R would equal two foods per

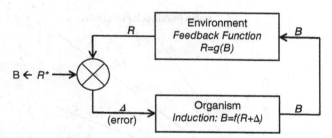

Figure 6.4 *The organism-environment feedback system explains activity rates maintained by ratio and interval schedules.* Note: The PIE rate (R) is compared with the set rate (R^*) that would induce the activity rate (B). The difference is Δ or error. In the organism, positive Δ increases activity rate and negative Δ decreases activity rate according to an induction function f. The activity rate impacts the environment according to a feedback function g, resulting in PIE rate R. In ratio schedules, Δ remains always either positive or negative, driving activity to the highest possible or to zero. For interval schedules, an activity rate exists for which Δ equals zero.

minute, but such a low peck rate would be induced by a lower food rate, say one food per minute—R^*—or, put another way, R of two per minute would induce a peck rate higher than 20—in this sense, R is too high for that B. So Δ ($R-R^*$) would be positive (equal to 1.0 in this example). For lines a, b, and c in Figure 6.3, Δ remains positive until activity rate reaches a physical upper limit where it can go no higher. For line d in Figure 6.3, Δ remains negative until activity rate decreases to zero. Thus ratio schedules generate either extremely high activity rates or none at all. Fruit pickers and gamblers work at furious rates or not at all.

Interval schedules delivering good PIEs generate moderate activity rates, comparable to checking or sampling if the outcome has become available. FI schedules rely on a clock to time out before activity produces the outcome. VI schedules often operate with a probability of setting up delivery every second or so. A setup probability of 1/60 every second generates a VI 1 minute. Much research has focused on VI schedules of food delivery in rats, monkeys, and pigeons. The top graph in Figure 6.2 shows performance on a VI 30 s and illustrates the moderate activity rate that such a schedule maintains. In contrast with the VR performance in the lower graph, where press rates ranged up to 90 per minute and averaged to 18, the press rates in the upper graph only ranged up to 13 per minute and averaged to 7 per minute.

Figure 6.5 shows feedback functions for five different VI schedules relating food rate to peck rate in pigeons. Each curve rises steeply for low peck rates and levels off near its maximum payoff rate as peck rate increases. The feedback system in Figure 6.4 helps to understand why interval schedules generate moderate activity rates. At low activity rates, R^* is low, R exceeds R^*, Δ is positive, and induction drives low activity rates higher, just as for a VR schedule. As activity rate increases, R^* increases while R approaches its upper limit, and at some moderate activity rate—call it B^*—R and R^* are equal. At that activity rate (B^*), Δ equals zero, and activity rate stabilizes around that activity rate, because higher activity rates than B^* cause Δ to be negative, and decrease B back toward B^*. Thus B stabilizes around B^*, because if B falls short of B^*, Δ is positive, increasing

Stability and Change

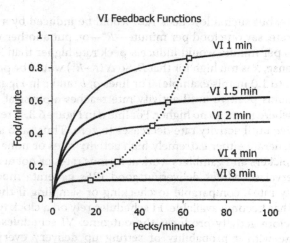

Figure 6.5 *Feedback functions for five VI schedules maintaining pecking with food inducers (PIEs). Note:* Each curve rises quickly at low activity rates and then flattens out as activity rate increases. At low activity rates, Δ in Figure 6.4 is positive, but as PIE rate flattens at higher activity rates, Δ decreases and becomes negative. The squares show typical stable activity rates where Δ equals zero. The dotted curve connects the squares, showing typical results from an experiment in which different VI schedules were presented until activity rate stabilized.

B, and if B exceeds B^*, Δ is negative, decreasing B; always bringing B back to B^*. The squares connected by the dotted lines show typical results of an experiment employing several different VI schedules, and in which activity rate is allowed to stabilize on each schedule. Stable activity level increases as the VI becomes richer, because the upper limit on payoff rate increases.

A full explanation of rates on interval and ratio schedules would take account of at least two additional factors. First, organisms tend to interact differently with interval schedules than with ratio schedules. For example, when food depends on a VI schedule pigeons peck at a key, whereas when food depends on a VR schedule they swipe at the key or nibble it. The different activity on the ratio schedule generates extremely high rates of key-switch operating. Second, the food maintaining the operant activity also induces some non-operant activity that competes with the operant activity and thus tends to lower the rate of the operant activity. A fuller treatment of pigeons' performances may be found in the paper by Baum and Grace (2020).

Figure 6.6 shows some data gathered from a rat's interactions with a lever that produced food pellets. The vertical axis shows lever-operation or "press" rate during an experimental session of about an hour. The horizontal axis shows consecutive sessions. The first set of circles shows press rate for a VI schedule. Three features deserve notice. First, press rate varied considerably from session to session. The drop after the first seven sessions resulted from a ten-day holiday between the seventh and eighth sessions. Second, despite the variability, trends appear clearly. The condition prior to the first VI condition maintained a lower press rate because activity-food covariance was less—half the pellets were produced by a press and half delivered without a press—and the switch to the VI caused press rate to increase. Third, press rate eventually stabilized—that is, after enough

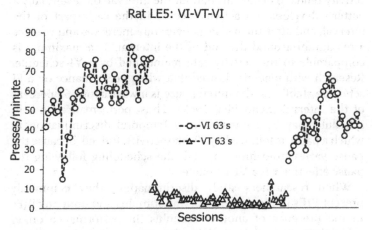

Figure 6.6 *Session-by-session activity rates in one rat exposed to VI, then VT, and then VI again.* Note: The first set of circles shows activity rate maintained by a VI 63 s schedule of food. The triangles show activity rate when covariance is removed: a VT 63 s schedule. The final set of circles shows activity rate when the VI schedule is reintroduced. Data are from the experiment by Baum and Aparicio (2020).

sessions, press rate ceased to exhibit a trend; it stabilized at about 70 per minute. The second set of press rates (triangles) shows the effect of eliminating the requirement of a press to produce food. With such a schedule, a *variable-time* (VT) schedule, food is delivered independently of the rat's activity; no covariance exists between pressing and food. Press rate dropped to a low level, but stabilized at about 4 presses per minute; the food still induced some interaction with the lever. The third set of press rates (circles) shows the effect of re-introducing the VI schedule. Press rate at once began to rise. Press rate in the second exposure to VI may have stabilized at a lower level than in the first exposure; more sessions would have been required to be sure. As the flattening feedback curves in Figure 6.5 show, above a moderately high level, activity rate may vary considerably without affecting PIE rate.

Performance on FI schedules differs from performance on VI schedules because the time interval that must pass is constant. In initial exposure to FI, an acquisition process occurs. At first, activity tends to occur throughout the interval, but eventually a pattern develops: no activity occurs in the early part of the interval, and after the pause, activity rate increases and reaches a maximum around the end of the interval. The maximum is comparable to the activity rate maintained by a VI schedule. Research with pigeons showed that when performance on a FI schedule stabilizes, the initial pause is always about 60 percent of the interval (Schneider, 1969). Thus, performance on a FI schedule may be compared to a temporal discrimination in which a pause is followed by VI-like activity. Indeed, because the pause varies from food to food, the scheduling following the pause effectively *is* a VI schedule.

When researchers study discrimination, they commonly present PIEs in the presence of one stimulus and omit any PIEs in the presence of another stimulus. In performance on FI schedules, no food is available for a time after the previous interval ended with food, and that regularity results in no activity being induced during the early part of the interval. Later times do induce activity, however. Thus, we may say that the temporal discrimination means that early times fail to induce activity whereas later times do. Another way to express the absence of activity when food is unavailable is to say that when food is unavailable, the activity extinguishes or is subject to extinction. Extinction occurs when the inducers that maintained an activity no longer occur. The activity decreases in time taken, and may even seem to drop out altogether. Figure 6.7 depicts extinction of a pigeon's pecking at a key trained in the laboratory by arranging that key pecking occasionally produced food (e.g., a VI schedule). On the left, we see the time allocation among key pecking, other food-related activities (e.g., moving about the chamber and pecking at the floor), and non-food-related activities (e.g., grooming). Key pecking takes up much time. The pie chart on the right shows time allocation after no food has occurred for a long time. Now key pecking and food-related activities take little time, and non-food-related activities (e.g., resting) take up most time. "Pausing," for example, in a FI schedule, means just that other activities fill the time.

Even though the activity virtually disappears, extinction does not mean the undoing of acquisition. Extinguished activities rarely disappear entirely. We see this clearly in the phenomenon of *reinstatement*. Suppose a pigeon is pecking at a key and the

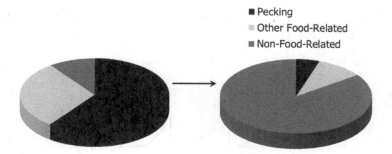

Figure 6.7 *The transition from food-maintained pecking to extinction as time allocation. Note:* **Left:** Pecking takes up the most time, followed by other food-related activities, both induced by the food. **Right:** In extinction, the absence of food reduces pecking and food-related activities to low levels, and other, non-food related activities take up most of the time.

pecking occasionally produces food on a VI schedule. Now, if the food ceases to be forthcoming, gradually the pecking ceases. Figure 6.8 depicts the results of an experiment. After training, pecks were occurring at a moderately high rate of about 50 per minute, and on the first day of extinction, 30 minutes passed with no food (Day 1). Pecking fell gradually to a low level. On Day 2, no food occurred for another 30 minutes. Although peck rate was close to zero at the end of Day 1's session, pecking started again on Day 2, but at a lower rate than at the start of Day 1's session. Pavlov reported this sort of overnight recovery and called it "spontaneous recovery." Subsequent research tied spontaneous recovery to the reintroduction of the experimental conditions after a night in the home cage. On Day 2, peck rate fell faster and all the way to zero. On Day 3, again no food occurred for 30 minutes. Pecking began at a low rate, dropped quickly to zero and remained there. Then, at the end of the 30 minutes, the researcher delivered some food independently of the pigeon's behavior. Immediately after the food, we see a burst of pecking. The delivery of food, all by itself, reinstated pecking. The food still induced pecking, despite the 90 minutes of extinction and reduction of peck rate to zero. Reinstatement was observed in pigeons, rats, and students (with tokens instead of food; Reid, 1958).

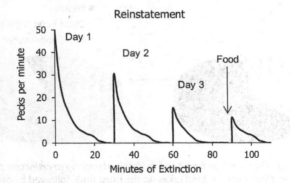

Figure 6.8 *Cartoon representation of* Reid's (1958) *experiment showing reinstatement. Note*: Three days of extinction preceded the test. Activity rate had decreased to zero. When food was presented, independent of behavior, the activity reinstated.

Persistence of induction even after extinction also applies to *resurgence*, the reappearance of an extinguished activity when alternative activities extinguish. Figure 6.9 shows how resurgence is studied in the laboratory. In Phase 1, a rat is trained to press a lever (A) by occasionally presenting food contingent on the pressing (e.g., on a VI schedule), and a second lever B never produces food. Pressing soon occurs only on lever A, at a stable moderate rate (e.g., 30 presses/min), and pressing lever A is the "target" activity. In Phase 2, food is discontinued for pressing lever A and is now available only for pressing lever B. Activity rate of pressing lever B increases while pressing lever A extinguishes. In Phase 3, food is discontinued for lever B as well as lever A. The result called resurgence appears as renewed pressing of lever A (solid line) while pressing lever B extinguishes (dashed line). Resurgence may model the reappearance of undesirable behavior after it has extinguished when induction of alternatives becomes weak. For example, suppose a person manages to quit a habit like smoking or nail-biting and instead chews gum. If chewing gum becomes unavailable, smoking or nail-biting may reappear.

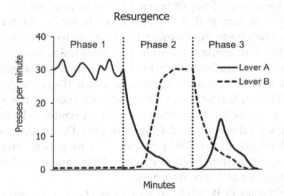

Figure 6.9 *Cartoon representation of an experiment on resurgence.*
Note: In Phase 1, only operating lever A produces food, and operating lever B has no effect. Activity focuses on lever A. In Phase 2, operating lever B produces food, and operating lever A has no effect. After a while, activity focuses on lever B. In Phase 3, neither lever produces food, and some activity on lever A resurges.

Experiments indicate that extinction constitutes formation of a discrimination between PIE (food) available and PIE (food) unavailable. For example, if one trains a pigeon's key pecking with a VI schedule, then unpredictably discontinues food, then trains again, then discontinues food again, and so on, repeatedly, extinction when food is discontinued becomes faster and faster. The situation resembles a pigeon foraging for seeds in a grass patch; eventually the seeds deplete, and the pigeon leaves. The shift resembles what happens if food is only available when the key is green and not when red: pecking at the red key decreases while pecking at the green key is maintained. Absence of food in the repeated-extinction procedure is like the red key. Pecking continues for a while, because only the absence of food distinguishes extinction from training, but after no food occurs for a while pecking ceases.

Further evidence that extinction is discrimination results when one varies the VI schedule in the training condition of the repeated-extinction procedure. The leaner the VI—that is, the longer the average time between food deliveries—the longer the time for the activity to extinguish (Baum, 2012). The discrimination that forms is between a certain food rate and a zero food rate. If the difference between food rates is large, extinction is fast, and if the difference is small, extinction is slower. The closer the training food rate is to zero, the more slowly the discrimination forms. The same holds for avoidance activity when avoidance is trained, then shock is discontinued, then avoidance is trained again, and so on (Boren & Sidman, 1957). During training, avoidance activity reduces the rate of shocks to a low level, so when shock is discontinued, that low rate must be discriminated from zero rate. Discrimination initially develops slowly. With repeated training and extinction, however, extinction becomes faster. Discrimination between low shock rate and zero improves.

Discrimination is rarely so simple as the red-key-green-key example, because what constitutes a stimulus is rarely so simple, as we see in the example of the repeated-extinction procedures, where discrimination is between different PIE rates. We will address the meaning of "stimulus" and discrimination further in the next chapter.

Further Reading

Baum, W. M. (2012). Extinction as discrimination. *Behavioural Processes, 90*(1), 101–110. This paper reports an experiment in which rate of extinction varied directly with food rate.

Baum, W. M., & Aparicio, C. F. (2020). Response-Reinforcer Contiguity versus Response-Rate-Reinforcer-Rate covariance in rats' lever pressing: Support for a multiscale view. *Journal of the Experimental Analysis of Behavior, 113*(3), 530–548.

Baum, W. M., & Grace, R. C. (2020). Matching theory and induction explain operant performance. *Journal of the Experimental Analysis of Behavior, 113*(2), 390–418.

Boren, J. J., & Sidman, M. (1957). A discrimination based upon repeated conditioning and extinction of avoidance behavior. *Journal of Comparative and Physiological Psychology, 50*(1), 18–22. Repeated alternation of avoidance training and extinction of avoidance resulted in faster extinction of avoidance.

Craig, A. R., Nall, R. W., Madden, G. J., & Shahan, T. A. (2016). Higher alternative non-drug reinforcement produces faster suppression of cocaine seeking but more resurgence when removed. *Behavioural Brain Research, 306*(1), 48–51. Rats were first trained to self-administer cocaine, then given an alternative that produced food, and then exposed to extinction of the food-producing alternative. Cocaine seeking decreased when food was available, but resurged when food was removed.

Ferster, C. B., & Skinner, B. F. (1957). *Schedules of reinforcement*. Appleton-Century-Crofts. This massive volume summarizes years of study of food-maintained activity with various schedules in pigeons.

Reid, R. L. (1958). The role of the reinforcer as a stimulus. *British Journal of Psychology, 49*(3), 202–209. An early report of reinstatement as a result of presentation of the inducing event that had maintained activity before extinction.

Schneider, B. A. (1969). A two-state analysis of fixed-interval responding in the pigeon. *Journal of the Experimental Analysis of Behavior, 12*(5), 677–687. A thorough investigation of activity patterns maintained by FI schedules.

7

Stimulus

In Latin, *stimulus* (plural *stimuli*) means "goad," adopted perhaps because early research on reflexes involved poking a frog's leg with a needle, but the meaning of stimulus gradually morphed into *any feature of the environment that induces activity in the organism* (as process). Even in Pavlov's experiments, tones and meat powder were inducers rather than goads. We have seen many examples in previous chapters—houses for a bear, person for a fish, a potential mate, snake eggs, and so on. Not every feature of the environment is a stimulus, however. To be a stimulus, a situation or an event must affect behavior.

To affect behavior, a feature of the environment must be able to interact with the organism's process; it must stimulate some sense organ. Pigeons' visual acuity is similar to humans', but different smells hardly serve to induce or not induce pigeons' key pecking. Visual displays only support simple discriminations of lever pressing in rats and dogs, but rats and dogs perform amazing feats of discrimination of smells. Dogs can tell from the smell of a woman's urine if she is pregnant or even if she has certain diseases. Rats have been trained to locate land mines by smell to help clear mine fields. Electric eels and other electric fish find prey by sensing disturbances in their electric field. Some birds navigate by the earth's magnetic field. If the organism is equipped to receive a feature of the environment, then that feature may become an inducer; otherwise not.

Introduction to Behavior: An Evolutionary Perspective, First Edition.
William M. Baum.
© 2024 John Wiley & Sons, Inc. Published 2024 by John Wiley & Sons, Inc.

Sometimes the inducing stimulus or inducer may be very specific. In experiments with male Stickleback fish, the territorial male attacks a male intruder but courts a female visitor. What distinguishes the male from the female? Experiments with models revealed that the red belly of the intruding male induced attack. Even a red disk bearing no resemblance to a fish induced attack when introduced into the male's territory. In contrast, the female's distended belly, which is not red, was the feature that induced courting. When pigeons are trained in a discrimination between a red triangle and a green circle, subsequent tests show that some pigeons discriminate on the basis of color and others on the basis of shape. Even though both features were in covariance with presence and absence of food, only one or the other became an inducer.

A stimulus must be in covariance with a PIE—positive or negative (Figure 3.2)—to become an inducer, but covariance alone is not sufficient, as the example of the red triangle and green circle shows. In that example, color and shape were redundant, and only one or the other mattered. In the example of the male Stickleback, many features that might have been inducers were actually irrelevant; only the shape and color of the belly mattered.

The distinction between features that matter to induction and features that are irrelevant applies to all discriminations. Food aversions, for example, occur when illness follows ingestion of a distinctive substance. Food aversions in rats depend only on the smell and taste of the food, whereas food aversions in pigeons depend on the visual appearance of the food. Both appearance and smell seem to induce aversion in humans.

Sometimes the exact features that are relevant and irrelevant may be difficult to specify, particularly in induction of *concepts*. Consider the following experiment by Herrnstein and Loveland (1964). A pigeon in a chamber with a small translucent screen for a key was shown slides on the screen. Each slide was presented for a minute, then another slide for a minute, and so on. If the pigeon pecked at the screen, operating the micro-switch, sometimes it got to eat a little grain. The pigeon was shown 80 slides per daily session, in random order. The researchers had thousands of slides from *National Geographic* and other sources. The slides showed scenes from all over the world—cities, forests, deserts, and jungles, with individuals, portions of individuals, and groups. Forty of the selected 80 slides contained a human, and the other 40 depicted similar scenes but with no humans. The pigeon only received food when the slide on the screen contained a human. After several sessions of exposure to this situation, pigeons began to peck more at the slides that contained a human. After more training, pecking only occurred when the slide contained a human. A discrimination formed between slides containing humans and those with no human. Then the researchers began showing the pigeons new slides that the pigeons had never seen before, hundreds of slides. The pigeons continued pecking only at the slides containing a human. The pigeons had acquired and were displaying the concept "human being."

What then is a concept? Subsequent experiments obtained similar results with the concepts "tree," "oak leaf," "fish," and a particular person (Herrnstein et al., 1976). In every experiment, the researchers could identify which slides were exemplars, and their judgments largely agreed with the pigeons'. So, the researchers and the pigeons both discriminated trees from bushes, oak leaves from other leaves, fish from other aquatic creatures, and a particular person seen in many different contexts and angles from other people. Thus, a concept, in behavioral terms, is a discrimination complex enough for humans to have difficulty identifying its defining features but which we humans are able to make nevertheless. Put succinctly, a concept is *appropriate response to novel instances*, where "appropriate" means what a human researcher would say.

Whatever features make a "human," many other features are irrelevant and do not matter. The setting—jungle or city—does not matter, whether in groups or not does not matter, and whether only partly visible does not matter. We and the pigeons still behave equivalently: the pigeon pecks and we say "human." Thus, all the slides with humans were equivalent, and all the slides without humans were equivalent as far as inducing similar activity or not.

In the pigeon experiment, these equivalences, sorting the slides into two categories, were trained. Presumably people also are trained to see others as "human." Historically such training has also worked to induce "human" only when looking at members of one's own tribe. Tribe members were all equivalent inducers of "human," and all others were equivalent inducers of "non-human." Saying "human" in the presence of *all* human beings may be a relatively recent development in human cultures and still in flux around the world.

Training equivalences is an inherent part of training any discrimination. Even in the relatively simple example of red key versus green key, the keys are seen from various angles and may fluctuate in brightness from time to time. The green key in covariance with a PIE like food induces pecking and is called a *discriminative stimulus*, symbolized as S^D. The red key not in covariance with food and that does not induce pecking is symbolized as S^Δ. In any discrimination S^D and S^Δ are not unique, but are *categories* of stimuli. A discrimination forms between two categories of stimuli, whether red-key views versus green-key views, food versus no food, or human versus non-human. Within a category, stimuli induce similar activity and may be called equivalent, or the activity may be said to *generalize* across stimuli. A discrimination consists of *generalization within categories and differentiation across categories*. Discriminating activity occurs equivalently (generalizes) within "human," "tree," "fish," or "that person," and differs between those categories and any others—for example, "human" versus "monkey" or "that person" versus someone else.

Understanding that discrimination occurs between categories helps to understand complex discriminations such as *relational* discriminations. Suppose a pigeon, monkey, or human is exposed to three keys or a screen on which circles are projected, as in Figure 7.1. When the circles are arranged as in Figure 7.1A, pecking or pressing on the right-hand smallest circle produces food, money, or approval, and choosing the other circles produces only a brief timeout. In another trial, Figure 7.1B, the circles change position, so that the discrimination must be based on size, not position. Now only choosing the middle circle, the

Stimulus | 77

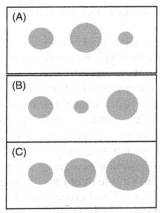

Figure 7.1 *A discrimination requiring relational behavior. Note:* In the top array (A), the correct choice—the smallest circle—is on the right. In the middle array (B), the correct choice is in the middle. In the bottom array (C), the correct choice is on the left and is one that was incorrect on earlier trials.

smallest, produces food, money, or approval. In Figure 7.1C, the smallest circle is now one that before would not have produced the PIE, and choosing the smallest circle alone pays off. Thus, the training requires that only the *smallest* circle in many such arrays of circles induces pecking or pressing. The discrimination cannot be based on absolute size or position. If the training succeeds, the whole array has to induce pecking or pressing the smallest circle. Researchers have had little success training relational discriminations in pigeons, but monkeys and humans acquire them readily. If a human or a monkey always chooses the smallest circle, responding appropriately to novel instances, we should say the human or monkey shows the concept "smallest" or "smaller than." Perhaps the training establishes three categories—smallest on the left, smallest on the right, and smallest in the middle—and within each category, all arrays are equivalent. Whatever the equivalences, the discrimination of smallest singles out size as a dimension, and discrimination occurs between different circle sizes. That interpretation raises further questions. What if the array included triangles? Would "smallest" generalize from circles to triangles? Humans have no trouble with this.

A way to train and study equivalence directly is the procedure *matching to sample*. In a typical procedure, a pigeon or human is first shown a visual stimulus—the sample—and then shown an array of choices ("comparisons") featuring different stimuli. To receive food, money, or praise, the participant (pigeon, adult, or child) must choose the stimulus in the array that the experimenter has designated as "correct." The task resembles a multiple-choice question that asks, "Which of the following statements is true?" and then presents a few possible answers. In a simple version, the sample might be a triangle or a square, the choice array might be red and green keys, and if the sample was a triangle, choosing a red key would be "correct," whereas if it was a square, choosing a green key would be "correct."

For humans, matching to sample may be complicated. An example is the task called "mental rotation." The samples are drawn from a pool of shapes, and a sample shape is presented along with a few choices, one of which is the same shape but rotated to a different angle of view and the other shapes are similar but not the same as the sample. Figure 7.2 shows an example. The sample is at the top, and the three choices are below. One is correct. More challenging examples employ representations of three-dimensional shapes. Experiments with pigeons show that pigeons can solve these "mental rotation" tasks when they receive food for correct choices (Hollard & Delius, 1982).

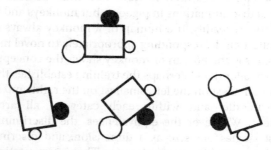

Figure 7.2 *A mental rotation task with sample above and choice array below. Note:* The correct choice is identical to the sample, but rotated. The other two differ from the sample.

Humans form equivalence classes extremely easily in matching to sample using abstract visual shapes. For example, suppose one has 12 different shapes and groups them into three sets of four: {A1, B1, C1, D1}, {A2, B2, C2, D2}, and {A3, B3, C3, D3}. A1, B1, and the rest are just various squiggles or designs. The trial types are shown in Table 7.1. When A1 is the sample, choosing B1 out of an array {B1, B2, B3} is correct, and B2 and B3 are incorrect. When A1 is the sample, choosing C1 out of an array {C1, C2, C3} is correct, and C2 and C3 are incorrect. When A1 is the sample, choosing D1 out of an array {D1, D2, D3} is correct and D2 and D3 are incorrect. After each choice trial, the person is told if the choice was "correct" or "incorrect." After correct choices are occurring regularly, equivalence is tested by presenting B1 as sample and {C1, C2, C3} as the comparison array, B1 as sample with {D1, D2, D3}, C1 as sample with {B1, B2, B3}, C1 as sample with {D1, D2, D3}, D1 as sample with {B1, B2, B3}, and D1 with {C1, C2, C3}. Equivalence means that B1 sample leads

Table 7.1 Matching-to-sample trials in training and testing equivalence.

Sample	Comparisons		
	Correct	Incorrect	Incorrect
Training Trials			
A1	B1	B2	B3
A1	C1	C2	C3
A1	D1	D2	D3
Equivalence Tests			
B1	C1	C2	C3
B1	D1	D2	D3
C1	B1	B2	B3
C1	D1	D2	D3
D1	B1	B2	B3
D1	C1	C2	C3

to choice of C1 and D1, C1 leads to choice of B1 and D1, and D1 leads to choice of B1 and C1. Undergraduates exposed to this training choose "correctly" (Table 7.1)—in accord with equivalence—in these equivalence tests.

Moreover, the participants choose according to equivalence in symmetry tests with, A1 as a comparison. For example, if presented with B1 as a sample and {A1, B2, B3} as comparisons, they chose A1. Thus, training just the sequences A1-B1, A1-C1, and A1-D1 sufficed to render all four shapes, A1, B1, C1, and D1, equivalent.

Matching to sample exemplifies the sort of complex discriminations that occur when most features of a situation remain constant and only certain specific features vary. In matching to sample, a trial consists always of a sample and a certain number of comparisons, and always just one of the comparisons is correct. Another example occurs when a monkey or human is presented with simple two-choice discriminations in which one alternative is always correct and the other always incorrect. In a study with monkeys, experimenters presented a monkey with a tray on which two distinct objects covered two wells (Harlow, 1949). If the monkey removed the object on one side, the well contained a raisin, which the monkey ate; if the monkey removed the other object, the well contained nothing. As soon as the monkey removed an object, the tray was removed and set up for the next trial. The experimenters were able to present new discriminations frequently, because they had a great many distinct objects. They presented each discrimination problem for six trials and then started a new one. On each of the six trials always the same object covered the raisin. Initially, the monkeys made errors in all six trials, but their performance changed as more discriminations were presented. After about 100 such discriminations, a definite pattern emerged: random choice on the first trial followed by perfect discrimination on the subsequent five trials. The researchers called this pattern a "learning set" or "learning to learn," but with the recognition that a PIE may serve as a stimulus, another interpretation is possible.

On the first trial with a new pair of objects, A and B, one of four possibilities occurs: (1) S^D, a discriminative stimulus, consisting of A and a raisin; (2) S^D consisting of B and a raisin; (3) S^Δ consisting of A and no food; and (4) S^Δ consisting of B and no food. Either S^D induces choice of that object for the subsequent five trials, and either S^Δ induces choice of the other object for the subsequent five trials. Such a pattern is commonly called "win-stay, lose-shift." In the natural world, foragers discovering prey in a patch or failing to discover any prey often exhibit such a pattern—staying in the patch or moving on.

Discrimination tasks fall into two categories: *successive* and *simultaneous*. In a successive discrimination, S^D and S^Δ are presented one after the other, not together, and discrimination is assessed by a difference in behavior—typically a difference in rate—between the two situations. One may think of the stimuli as different contexts in which different covariances occur. S^D signifies positive covariance between that stimulus and a good PIE like food or negative covariance between that stimulus and a bad PIE like injury, and S^D induces appropriate behavior. S^Δ signifies less covariance or none at all, and S^Δ induces other behavior. In the experiment with pigeons showing discrimination between human present (S^D) and no human present (S^Δ), discrimination was successive, because slides were presented one at a time, and pecking rate was high when the slide contained a person and low when the slide did not. Successive discriminations often are called *multiple schedules*. The person/no person experiment may be called a multiple VI Extinction schedule, because pecking produced food according to a VI in one context and pecking was ineffective in the other context. More generally, a multiple schedule presents two or more schedules, each in its own context. For example, a multiple VI 30 s FR 50 with pigeons might present the VI with a green key for two minutes and the FR with a red key for two minutes, in alternation. Each schedule occurs in a different context (key color), and the context induces activity according to that schedule. In this example, pecking at the green key occurs at a moderately high and constant rate, whereas pecking at the red key occurs at an extremely high rate, with some pausing before the ratio is executed. As the covariance varies from one context to the other, the performance induced varies also.

The person/no person experiment could have employed simultaneous discrimination, had the chamber included two screens, one with a slide containing a human and one without. Subsequent research did that with a variety of categories, such as flowers and cats (Bhatt et al., 1988). In a simultaneous discrimination, researchers likely will apply the words "choose" and "choice," because two or more alternatives are present. When two or more alternatives are simultaneous and each one pays off, doesn't pay off, or pays off according to a different schedule, the alternatives constitute *concurrent schedules*. For example, in a mental-rotation task, one alternative pays off, say, on a FR 1 (each time the correct alternative shape is picked, a payoff occurs), whereas the others produce no payoff. This trivial example, would be concurrent FR 1 Extinction. Suppose instead, a pigeon faces two keys, one on the left and one on the right (Figure 5.7), and pecks at the left key pay off according to a VI 30 s schedule while pecks at the right key pay off according to a FR 50. The two alternatives maintain different patterns of activity, but now these patterns may not be entirely independent of one another. For example, to receive the most food, most activity should go to the FR to earn a high food rate there, whereas the VI needs only to be sampled from time to time. We will take up choice and concurrent schedules in the next chapter.

Further Reading

Bhatt, R. S., Wasserman, E. A., Reynolds, W. F., jr., & Knauss, K. F. (1988). Conceptual behavior in the pigeon: Categorization of both familiar and novel examples from four classes of natural and artificial stimuli. *Journal of Experimental Psychology: Animal Behavior Processes, 14*(3), 219–234. This paper reports an experiment in which pigeons categorized images by pecking and getting food for "correct" choices (choices agreeing with the experimenters' judgments).

Harlow, H. F. (1949). The formation of learning sets. *Psychological Review, 56*(1), 51–65. The study with monkeys in which most features of the experiment remained the same across discrimination problems and food or no food on the first trial of a problem served as one cue in inducing correct choices in subsequent trials.

Herrnstein, R. J., & Loveland, D. H. (1964). Complex visual concept in the pigeon. *Science, 146*(3643), 549–551. A classic paper reporting acquisition of the concept "human being" in pigeons.

Herrnstein, R. J., Loveland, D. H., & Cable, C. (1976). Natural concepts in pigeons. *Journal of Experimental Psychology: Animal Behavior Processes, 2*(4), 285–302. Further testing of pigeons' ability to form complex concepts.

Hollard, V. D., & Delius, J. D. (1982). Rotational invariance in visual pattern recognition in pigeons and humans. *Science, 218*(4574), 804–806. Comparing humans' and pigeons' solutions to mental rotation problems.

8

Choice and Balance

Every activity, whether serving a tennis ball, driving to work, baking a cake, or writing an essay, consists of parts—also activities—that must work together harmoniously to produce a successful outcome. Each part must function together with the others in the same way that the pieces of a puzzle together define a whole or the organs function together to sustain the living organism. Successful working means that the parts of a process must not only be correct, but must coordinate their timing. If tossing the tennis ball takes too long, bringing the racquet down on it will not work with it correctly. If I take a wrong turn when driving to work, I will be delayed and late for work. If I fail to mix baking powder in the batter or put in too much, the activity will not result in a good cake. Organizing an essay requires adequate time spent in its various parts. If any part fails or functions incorrectly, the whole fails or functions incorrectly. The activity fails to achieve its goal: the tennis serve lands inaccurately; I arrive at work late; the cake is inedible; the essay is disorganized. Successful working requires balance among the parts of the activity. That balance may be expressed as a balance of times taken by the various parts.

In skilled activities like serving a tennis ball, timing is everything, but timing matters also on longer time scales. A bird foraging in an open area divides its time between searching for food and watching out for predators—eat, but not be eaten. Search and vigilance are parts of an overall pattern of activity ("foraging"), and each activity-part takes up some time.

Introduction to Behavior: An Evolutionary Perspective, First Edition.
William M. Baum.
© 2024 John Wiley & Sons, Inc. Published 2024 by John Wiley & Sons, Inc.

Choice and Balance

The parts of an activity must function together and within a certain time frame, because time is always limited. Serving a tennis ball takes up seconds only, and serving as part of playing tennis takes up only a small portion of the time taken by a game. A game takes up a portion of the time taken by a match. A tennis match takes up a small portion of a player's life. The amount of time taken is limited at every time scale, whether the serve, the game, the match, or the lifetime.

Even though all activities at a certain time scale all must coordinate together, they also compete for the limited time available. Balance occurs because each activity-part is constrained by the demands of the other activity-parts. Searching for food and watching out for predators compete with one another, but the situation induces both: presence of food induces search; open area induces vigilance. They compete because the limited time dictates that if one increases the other must decrease. More danger of predators induces more vigilance and less searching. Higher density of food induces more searching and less vigilance. The two activities exist in a dynamic tension with one another.

Competition and balance occur because every activity is induced by some feature of the environment—by some inducing stimulus or inducer. The inducers of working differ from the inducers for interacting with friends and family. All the activities that occur in a given time frame exist in dynamic tension with one another. All the competing and inducing result in an allocation of time among activities that inspires a pie chart like those in Chapter 5. Figure 8.1 illustrates time allocation and its relation to induction. The chart on the left illustrates allocation among several activities. The chart on the right shows the relative level of induction of the activities. The two charts match—that is, relative time taken by any activity (B_i) equals its relative level of induction (V_i). If the relative level of induction of an activity shifts, the proportion of time the activity takes shifts with it, but some other activities must shift too, because the organism's activities take up all the time available, and if one increases, others must decrease. If the demands of work increase, relative level of induction increases, and time spent working increases, but time spent in other activities such as being with

Choice and Balance | 87

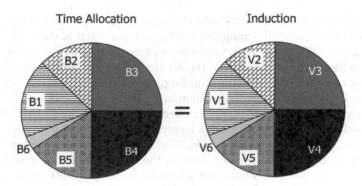

Figure 8.1 *Visual Representation of the Law of Allocation*. Note: The pie chart on the left represents the allocation or distribution of time among six activities: B1—B6. The pie chart on the right represents the relative competitive weights of the six activities: V1—V6. The Law of Allocation says that these two relative distributions are equal or match.

family and friends must decrease, and their relative level of induction decreases. If one activity increases its slice of the pie—the time available—other activities' slices must decrease.

The mathematical expression of this matching relation is:

$$\frac{B_j}{\sum_{i=1}^{n} B_i} = \frac{V_j}{\sum_{i=1}^{n} V_i} \qquad (8.1)$$

Equation 8.1 states that for any Activity j among n activities (6 activities in Figure 8.1), the proportion of time taken by Activity j out of the total time available (sum of the Bs) equals the level of induction of Activity j relative to the sum total of the levels of induction of all n activities. The equation captures the competition among activities. For this reason, V_i is called the "competitive weight" of Activity i.

What determines the competitive weight of an activity? Some inducers are more powerful than others—for example, the needs of a child versus your own entertainment. Beyond these differences, the level of induction of an activity depends on at least three factors: (a) the rate of the inducer (food, social contact, predator, injury); (b) the amount or magnitude of the inducer; and (c) the immediacy of the inducer—that is, the tightness of its covariance with the activity. The more often an inducer occurs, the more of the activity it induces—think of rate of encountering prey while hunting, rate of gambling payoffs, or avoidance in relation to rate of injuries. If an inducer can vary in amount, the more of it per occurrence the more of the activity it will induce—think of food (a larger prey versus a smaller prey) or injury (minor versus major). The tighter the covariance between the inducer and the activity, the more it will induce the activity—think of weight loss in relation to dieting (loose) versus the instant taste of ice cream (tight), or goods promised (loose) versus goods delivered (tight). Although difficult to assess in the everyday world, in the laboratory, where these factors may be measured and varied, they are often the focus of research.

In the laboratory, researchers try to discover the quantitative basis of competitive weight in Equation 8.1. As in all scientific research, we begin with the simplest possible situation and build from there. Much research has focused on choice between just two alternatives, although a few experiments have studied three, four, and eight alternatives. To get an idea how Equation 8.1 may be quantified, we may look at results with just two alternatives. A result that has been replicated many times in experiments that varied rate, amount, and immediacy is expressed in the following equation:

$$\frac{B_1}{B_2} = b\left(\frac{X_1}{X_2}\right)^s \qquad (8.2)$$

In Equation 8.2, B_1 and B_2 represent activity time taken by Alternatives 1 and 2, measured in time or switch operations estimating time, and X_1 and X_2 represent the two rates, amounts, or immediacies of the inducers, which are often food, sometimes water, and, for humans, money or points exchangeable for money. The parameter b estimates any bias that might favor one alternative over the other, apart from X_1 and X_2. If b equals 1.0, choice is unbiased and affected only by the ratio of X_1 to X_2. The parameter S estimates the sensitivity of choice to the ratio of X_1 to X_2. If b and S both equaled 1.0, then Equation 8.2 would state that the choice ratio equals the ratio of X_1 to X_2 and would be called "strict matching," but S often falls short of 1.0, a result called "undermatching." When analyzing the results of an experiment, researchers work with the logarithm of Equation 8.2:

$$log\left(\frac{B_1}{B_2}\right) = s \cdot log\left(\frac{X_1}{X_2}\right) + logb \qquad (8.3)$$

The advantage of Equation 8.3 is that it conforms to the equation for a straight line: $Y = S \cdot X + Y_0$, where Y is $log\left(\frac{B_1}{B_2}\right)$, X is $log\left(\frac{X_1}{X_2}\right)$, and Y_0 is $logb$. When the behavior ratio $\left(\frac{B_1}{B_2}\right)$ is plotted against the inducement ratio $\left(\frac{X_1}{X_2}\right)$ in logarithmic coordinates, the matching relation in Equation 8.2 appears as a straight line.

Figure 8.2 shows some examples of results from experiments with pigeons. Panel A shows the results of an experiment with a flock of wild pigeons. The apparatus arranged that only one pigeon at a time had access to two keys and a food hopper. The graph shows the ratio of all the pigeons' pecks at the two keys as a function of the rate ratio of food earned at the two keys. Five pairs of VI schedules were presented, each for weeks at a time until day-to-day choice stabilized. The equation indicates that the stable behavior ratios approximately matched the food ratios, because the exponent 1.06 is close to 1.0. Panel B shows results of a similar experiment, in which an individual pigeon (51RP) lived in a chamber and earned all its food by pecking at two keys, each paying off according to a VI schedule. Each point represents a day's activity ratio. Seven pairs of VI schedules were presented. The exponent 0.91 again is close to 1.0. Panel D shows the same sort of experiment as in Panel B, except that the inducer delivered according to the two VI schedules was water, instead of food. Again the exponent 1.02 is close to 1.0. Panel C shows typical results from a pigeon (P26) in an experiment in which the pigeon pecked at the two keys for about one hour a day. The unusual aspect of this experiment is that the inducement ratio was varied over an extremely wide range, from about

Choice and Balance

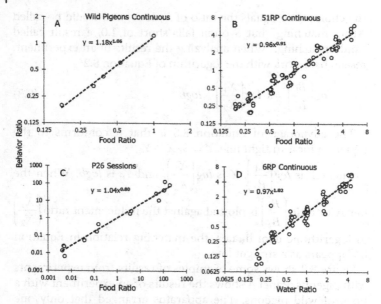

Figure 8.2 *Results of Four Experiments Studying Choice with Concurrent VI Schedules in Pigeons. Note*: **A**: a group of wild pigeons pecking one at a time (Baum, 1974). **B**: one pigeon living continuously in the experiment and operating two keys for all of its food (Baum, 1972). **C**: one pigeon exposed to daily sessions (Baum et al., 1999). **D**: one pigeon living continuously in the experiment and earning all of its water by operating the two keys (unpublished). Equations of the power functions appear near them. Note logarithmic axes.

1:200 to about 200:1. The exponent 0.8 falls short of 1.0, the result called "undermatching." Choice was less sensitive to the food ratio because relatively too much activity occurred for the lower-rate alternative.

This matching relation has been found, not just in pigeons, but in many species: mice, rats, monkeys, horses, possums, other birds, fish, and even insects. Figure 8.3 shows an example from an experiment with humans (undergraduate students). The task resembled a primitive video game in which alien space ships were to be detected and destroyed. Across a table, the person faced a large milk Plexiglas screen, behind which at three

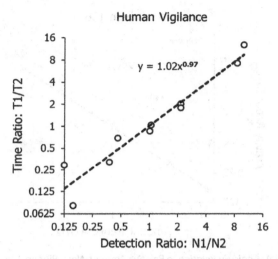

Figure 8.3 *Choice in a Vigilance Task with a Human Being. Note*: Participant detected "space ships" in two "areas" by pressing and holding two keys. Relative time watching is shown as a function of relative detections in the two areas. Note logarithmic axes. Data from Baum (1975).

locations lights were mounted. Two telegraph keys on the table could be pressed and held one at a time. When one key was held, alien ships appeared as red squares. When the other key was held, alien ships appeared as green squares. When a ship appeared, the person destroyed it by pushing a button: the ship flashed white and disappeared. Appearances of the ships were programmed according to two VI schedules that changed every other session. Figure 8.3 shows the ratio of time holding the two telegraph keys as a function of the ratio of detections (inducers; alien ships destroyed). The exponent of 0.97 and coefficient of 1.02 indicate that choice—the time ratio—almost exactly matched the ratio of inducers—an exponent of 1.0 and bias of 1.0 (strict matching).

Another variable one would expect to influence competitive weight (V) is amount—amount of food or money delivered on payoff. Suppose X in Equation 8.3 were amount, how would differences in amount affect choice? In one experiment, Landon et al.

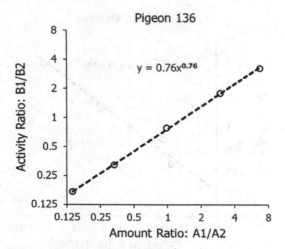

Figure 8.4 *Choice in Relation to Relative Amount. Note*: Pigeon 136 operated two keys producing different amounts of food. Note logarithmic axes. Data from Landon et al. (2003).

(2003) varied the amount of grain that pigeons could eat from the raised food hopper on payoff. The pigeons pecked at two keys that paid off according to equal VI schedules. Figure 8.4 shows the results for one pigeon, and the other five pigeons' results were similar. The matching relation was well-supported by the results, but the exponent or sensitivity (*S* in Equations 8.2 and 8.3) to amount ratio (0.76) was considerably less than 1.0. Although experiments on sensitivity to amount ratio have often found sensitivity to amount ratio to be lower than sensitivity to rate ratio, sensitivity in Figure 8.2C was about the same as in Figure 8.4, at 0.8.

Experiments have also addressed the effects of a delay or time penalty on choice. In this context "delay" means a signaled period of time that must elapse between effective activity and the delivery of the inducer. Such a delay entails waiting, as when you wait for an elevator after pressing the button or wait to be summoned at the doctor's office. The delay is re-expressed as *immediacy*, $\dfrac{1}{D_0 + D}$, for two reasons. First, one would like the variable X in Equations 8.2 and 8.3 to vary positively with competitive weight (V), and delay is a disadvantage, whereas immediacy is an advantage. Second, when inducers are tangibles like food or money, delay of delivery never actually equals zero; delivery takes a little time, so some minimal delay always intervenes, and that minimal delay is represented by D_0.

The results of a study of the effects of immediacy on choice appear in Figure 8.5. Pigeons pecked at two keys that paid off according to two equal VI schedules. When a key produced food, delivery of the food followed only after a period of time during which all lights were out ("blackout"). The researchers varied the durations of these blackouts at the two alternatives. Figure 8.5 shows that the activity ratio approximately matched the ratio of the immediacies, with sensitivity (1.11) only slightly greater than 1.0.

What if two alternatives differ in more than one of the three inducer variables? Suppose, for example, one alternative paid off a large amount but with a delay, whereas the other paid off a

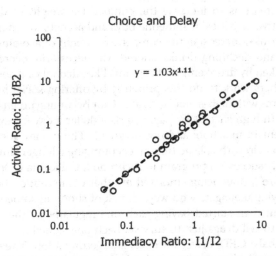

Figure 8.5 *Choice in Relation to Relative Immediacy. Note*: Pigeons operated two keys that produced food after different durations of blackout delay. Each point represents an average of six pigeons' data. Note logarithmic axes. Data from Chung and Herrnstein (1967).

small amount but with no delay. How would one predict choice? The simplest way that the three inducer variables—rate, amount, and immediacy—could combine to affect choice would be for the three power functions, as in Equation 8.2, to just multiply together:

$$\frac{B_1}{B_2} = b\left(\frac{R_1}{R_2}\right)^s \left(\frac{A_1}{A_2}\right)^a \left(\frac{I_1}{I_2}\right)^d \quad (8.4)$$

where S is sensitivity to rate ratio, a is sensitivity to amount ratio, and d is sensitivity to immediacy ratio. Some research has supported multiplying the power function for rate times the power function for amount, and some research has supported multiplying the function for amount times the function for immediacy. More research remains to be done.

Equations 8.1 to 8.4 imply one practical conclusion for changing the behavior of individuals and even communities—therapy and public policy. If you want to decrease some undesirable activity like taking illicit drugs or selling such drugs, a good way to achieve the decrease is to increase the competitive weight of desirable alternative activities. If someone buys and accepts too many alcoholic drinks, increasing the competitive weight of avoiding liquor stores and declining drinks offered will necessarily decrease the time taken by drunkenness. Programs like Alcoholics Anonymous and others work to do this primarily by offering social inducers. Programs with high-school girls at risk for becoming pregnant have met with high success by paying girls a dollar a day for every day they remain in school and not pregnant. The money goes into a fund to help with college tuition, encouraging a longer timeframe. A highly successful program in Richmond, California ("Operation Ceasefire"), now being emulated in other communities, began by identifying teenagers who were at risk of shooting someone. The program then started paying each one regularly, so they weren't forced to sell drugs just to survive. Each one signed a contract to meet goals: GED, driver's license, and getting a job. They met in groups and also received individual counseling. Most reached the goals, and the city experienced a large drop in gun violence. Equation 8.1 tells us that if you want to reduce crime in a neighborhood, the answer is not to add more police and crack down, but to provide attractive alternatives like well-maintained community centers where people socialize and play games. Improving quality of life in low-income communities means that the relative competitive weight of criminal activity would be driven down, and crime would be less of a problem.

Self-Control

Much dysfunctional behavior arises from the conflict between immediate results versus long-term results. On one hand, declining an offer of cake might be uncomfortable in the short-term, but on the other hand the inducement of good health would be greater in the long-term. Put another way, eating a piece of cake now has a nice immediate result, but in a longer timeframe avoiding sweets will bring about the greater result of good health.

The conflict of timeframes inspires research with human participants that investigates the tradeoff between amount and delay. People are given hypothetical choices between amounts (money, cigarettes, and other goods) postponed for various time periods versus an amount they might have immediately. For example, a participant might be offered a choice between $500 now versus $1000 in a month, but the participant actually receives neither. The "delay" of a month is not a delay in the earlier sense, because even if it were real, the person would not remain for a month in the laboratory, but would go on about life for the month. So the hypothetical "delay" is really a hypothetical postponement. The experiments are intended to address questions about short-term choice versus long-term choice, although the alternatives are often labeled "impulsiveness" and "self-control" on the assumption that preferring a small immediate amount over a large postponed amount would be impulsive, and that choosing the large postponed amount would be self-control. The choices are analogous to squandering money versus saving or taking addictive drugs versus abstaining. Choosing the short-term alternative offers small inducements that favor that activity in a small timeframe, whereas choosing the long-term alternative offers large inducements that favor that activity in a long timeframe, in the long run.

A typical experiment begins by offering the participant a choice between $500 now versus $500 in a month. The participant chooses $500 now. The immediate amount is lowered for the next choice offered, say to $490. As long as the participant chooses the immediate amount, it is decreased, until finally the immediate amount is small enough that the person chooses $500 in a month. On the next trial, the immediate amount is increased. This process is repeated until the researchers have an estimate of the immediate amount that is equally likely to be chosen as the postponed $500—the indifference point. Then the researchers offer $500 postponed for a different period of time, say, six months. The indifference point will be for a smaller immediate amount. Then they offer $500 postponed for a week, and the indifference point will be for a larger immediate amount. When the researchers have determined several indifference points, they plot a curve showing immediate amount versus postponement interval for these indifference points. Such a curve is called a "discounting function." An example appears in Figure 8.6,

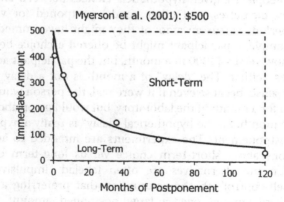

Figure 8.6 *Temporal Discounting of Money with a Standard Amount of $500. Note:* The curve fitted to the points represents indifference between an immediate amount on the vertical axis and $500 postponed for durations along the horizontal axis. It divides the space into two areas: one in which the long-term alternative is chosen and one in which the short-term alternative is chosen. The steeper the curve the more discounting. Data from Myerson et al. (2001).

which shows indifference points between immediate amounts of money and $500 postponed for various lengths of time. The fitted curve divides the space into two areas. Above the curve are immediate amounts that would be preferred—short-term choosing. Below the curve are immediate amounts that would be rejected in favor of the postponed amount—long-term choosing. The ratio of the area under the curve to the area above the curve would be an indicator of preference for long-term choosing over short-term choosing. The greater the area under the curve, the less discounting and the more self-control.

Even though the choices are hypothetical and rely of the participants' verbal competence, imagination, and upbringing, the same mathematical formulation of matching applies, Equation 8.4 with just amount and immediacy. From this equation, one derives an equation to describe the indifference points:

$$A_I = \frac{A_P}{(1+kT)^U} \quad (8.5)$$

where A_I is the immediate amount, A_P is the postponed amount, T is the postponement duration, and U is the ratio of exponents a/d in Equation 8.4. The curve in Figure 8.6 represents this equation.

Research on discounting has produced some striking and potentially useful results. For example, people who are addicted to drugs like heroin and nicotine discount money more steeply than non-addicted people. Some research suggests that the parameters k and U of Equation 8.5 may be enduring individual traits.

Group Foraging

Another area of research in which power functions like Equation 8.2 enter is the study of organisms' aggregation in groups or flocks. Suppose two locations (called "patches") contain a resource—say, food (called "prey")—and multiple foragers may go to exploit those patches. If the two patches were equivalent, we might expect equal numbers of foragers to congregate in them. Suppose, however, that the rate of encountering prey is greater in one patch than the other. Then we expect more foragers to go to the richer patch. The equation that applies is:

$$\frac{N_1}{N_2} = b\left(\frac{R_1}{R_2}\right)^s \qquad (8.6)$$

where N_1 and N_2 are the numbers of foragers congregating in Patch 1 and Patch 2, R_1 and R_2 are the rates of encountering prey, s is sensitivity of the group to the resource ratio (R_1 to R_2), and b is bias toward one patch or the other due to factors other than the resource ratio. Equation 8.6 is called the *Ideal Free Distribution*, because it describes how foraging organisms distribute themselves between patches when they are free to move and no environmental factors interfere.

The Ideal Free Distribution has been studied in a variety of species, mostly birds and fishes. Figure 8.7 shows the results of

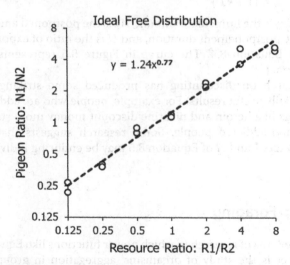

Figure 8.7 *Ideal Free Distribution in a Flock of Pigeons.* Note: Pigeons distributed themselves between two patches with different rates of delivering prey. The ratio of pigeons is shown as a function of the resource ratio. Note logarithmic axes. Data from Bell and Baum (2002).

an experiment by Ken Bell with a flock of 34 pigeons. The two patches were two squares of carpeting. The prey were dried peas and were delivered via tubes to the patches. The rate of delivery at the lean patch was a fraction of rate at the rich patch. As soon as a pea arrived, one or another pigeon snapped it up. The pigeons were extremely active, but some stayed put in one or the other patch while some switched patches repeatedly. Even so, after a couple of minutes, the numbers of pigeons on the two patches stabilized. Figure 8.7 shows the ratio of pigeons at the two patches as a function of the ratio of delivery rates, the resource ratio. The pigeons distributed themselves according to Equation 8.6, but the exponent 0.77 fell short of 1.0, indicating that relatively too many pigeons stayed on the leaner patch. The experiment took no account of dominance relations among the flock, and possibly more dominant pigeons went to the richer patch and excluded some subordinate pigeons.

A few studies have attempted to study the Ideal Free Distribution with human participants. One experiment by John Kraft, included in his doctoral research, arranged situations in which undergraduates in a group could earn points exchangeable for cash. In one experiment, 17 undergraduates were exposed to a situation where they could sit in either of two rows of 20 chairs. Each row had a designated total number of points throughout a block of 26 trials. Each individual received points on a trial equal to the total designated for their row divided by the number of people in the row. For example, if the resource ratio was 50:10, and 12 people sat in the 50 row, those people earned 4.17 points, whereas the five people in the other row earned 2 points. After initially taking seats and hearing the points earned, the participants were allowed to switch rows. Then a new trial began. After 26 trials with that resource ratio, a new block began with a new resource ratio. After several trials, the numbers in each row stabilized for the rest of the trial block. Figure 8.8A shows the stable participant ratios after switching as a function of resource ratio. The results resemble the results with pigeons in Figure 8.7. With an exponent of 0.79, some undermatching occurred, indicating a relative excess of people in the leaner patch (row).

100 | Choice and Balance

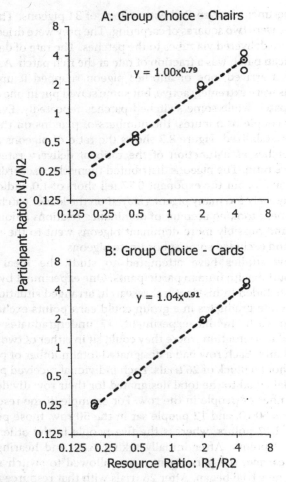

Figure 8.8 *Ideal Free Distribution in Groups of Human Participants*. Note: **A**: participants distributed themselves between two rows of chairs. Each row was delegated a certain number of points, and the ratio of delegated points constituted the resource ratio. **B**: participants chose between red cards and blue cards instead of moving between rows of chairs. Note logarithmic axes. Data from Kraft and Baum (2001) and Kraft's doctoral dissertation at the Psychology Department, University of New Hampshire (1999).

Figure 8.8B shows results from another of Kraft's experiments. Groups of 10–12 undergraduates sat around a large table, and each participant held two cards, one red and one blue. The procedure was the same as with the chairs, except that on each trial a participant held up either the red card or the blue card, instead of sitting in one or the other row of chairs. Eight blocks of 40 trials were conducted. As before, participants were given the opportunity to switch in each trial. Figure 8.8B shows the stable participant ratios after switching as a function of resource ratio. This time, the exponent comes close to perfect matching, with an exponent of 0.91.

All of the experiments reviewed in this chapter together support the idea of power-function induction expressed in Equation 8.2. As is always true in any science, only further research will tell if this formulation is correct. Any of these experiments could suggest other experiments to test the concepts further.

Further Reading

Baum, W. M. (1972). Choice in a continuous procedure. *Psychonomic Science, 28*(5), 263–265. Some results appear in Figure 8.2B.

Baum, W. M. (1974). Choice in free-ranging wild pigeons. *Science, 185*(4145), 78–79. Some results appear in Figure 8.2A.

Baum, W. M. (1975). Time allocation in human vigilance. *Journal of the Experimental Analysis of Behavior, 23*(1), 45–53. Results for one participant appear in Figure 8.3.

Baum, W. M., Schwendiman, J. W., & Bell, K. E. (1999). Choice, contingency discrimination, and foraging theory. *Journal of the Experimental Analysis of Behavior, 71*(3), 355–373. Results for one pigeon appear in Figure 8.2C.

Bell, K. E., & Baum, W. M. (2002). Group foraging sensitivity to predictable and unpredictable changes in food distribution: Past experience or present circumstances? *Journal of the Experimental Analysis of Behavior, 78*(2), 179–194. Some results appear in Figure 8.7.

Chung, S. H., & Herrnstein, R. J. (1967). Choice and delay of reinforcement. *Journal of the Experimental Analysis of Behavior, 10*(1), 67–74. Average results appear in Figure 8.5.

Kraft, J. R., & Baum, W. M. (2001). Group choice: The ideal free distribution of human social behavior. *Journal of the Experimental Analysis of Behavior, 76*(1), 21–42. Some results appear in Figure 8.8.

Landon, J., Davison, M., & Elliffe, D. (2003). Concurrent schedules: Reinforcer magnitude effects. *Journal of the Experimental Analysis of Behavior, 79*(3), 351–365. Results for one pigeon appear in Figure 8.4.

Myerson, J., Green, L., & Warusawitharana, M. (2001). Area under the curve as a measure of discounting. *Journal of the Experimental Analysis of Behavior, 76*(2), 235–243. An experiment on temporal discounting discussed in connection with Figure 8.6.

9

Verbal Behavior and Rules

Defining verbal behavior is difficult because verbal behavior is not cleanly distinct from other behavior. An approximate definition is that verbal behavior is induced partly by the presence of another person, called the *listener*, who responds to the stimuli generated by the speaker's behavior. Researchers commonly add that the speaker and listener belong to the same *verbal community*. This addition aims to rule out non-operant ("instinctive") behavior, as when a male song bird patrols its territory while singing, and other males (would-be listeners) respond by singing back and remaining in their territories. Although the line between operant and instinctive behavior is blurry, for the sake of clarity, we focus on human verbal behavior.

Even restricting ourselves to human verbal behavior, complexities arise. First, verbal behavior does not just refer to speech; it is not necessarily vocal. It includes signing and gestures and thus may depend on visual cues, not just auditory. If Tom and Jane are at the dining table, and Tom points to the salt, and Jane passes the salt, Tom's gesture counts as verbal behavior. To keep discussion simple, we might still call Tom the speaker and Jane the listener. It does not matter whether Tom points or says, "Please pass the salt," because these are equivalent in their effect on the listener's behavior (Jane passes the salt).

Equivalence is fundamental to verbal behavior, just as to other operant behavior. When a rat procures food by operating a lever, the rat does so in a variety of ways—biting, licking, pawing—all

Introduction to Behavior: An Evolutionary Perspective, First Edition.
William M. Baum.
© 2024 John Wiley & Sons, Inc. Published 2024 by John Wiley & Sons, Inc.

of which are equivalent in their effect: operating the lever and producing the food. Similarly, with verbal behavior, Tom may induce Jane's passing the salt in a variety of ways: "Salt, please" or "May I have the salt?" and so on. They are all parts of the activity of "getting Jane to pass the salt."

Equivalence is not infinite, however, because the past experiences of the speaker and listener matter too. If Tom spoke to Jane in Russian and Jane does not understand Russian, Jane will not respond. If Tom and Jane have a history in which Tom has offended Jane, Jane may refuse to pass the salt. Like all operant behavior, verbal behavior depends for its induction and its effects on past history.

At least some of the two interlocutors' history implies belonging to a verbal community. Young children abandoned in the forest who survive—called "feral" children—have never been found to speak when they are captured. The language you speak and that you speak at all depend on your interactions with a verbal community. We may define a verbal community as a group of potential listeners and speakers all of whom interact with some other members over the course of time. A child growing up in a verbal community interacts with some but not necessarily all community members, as is true of any member.

Not only does history with a verbal community matter, but the same vocalization may have different effects on the listener, depending on the speaker's movements ("body language") and the context. Saying "water" might result in the listener's passing the water, might prompt the listener to fetch a mop, or might prompt the listener to respond "H2O." So, the listener is necessary for verbal behavior, but is only part of the environmental context that induces the speaker's verbal behavior.

Skinner (1957), who invented the concept of verbal behavior as a way to understand phenomena that usually go under the rubric "language," in trying to identify varieties of verbal behavior defined several discrete verbal units, most notably ones that he called "mand" and "tact." A mand is a bit of verbal behavior in which action has a specific result. Tom's asking for the salt would be a mand, defined by its getting Jane to pass the salt. A tact is a bit of verbal behavior that is principally induced by some feature of the environment, like "That puddle is water" or "What a nice day!" The difference between a mand and a tact is not clear-cut. If you say, "What a nice day," and I do not respond, you may be offended because the appropriate listener response is something like, "Yes, isn't it?" Though "What a nice day" may seem like a tact, it is supposed to produce a specific result. If Jane says to Tom, "I love you," is that a mand or a tact?

Most research on verbal behavior has focused on finding methods for training mands and tacts in developmentally disadvantaged children. This work has yielded many effective techniques that applied behavior analysts use. To be sure, successful navigation of everyday life depends on these basic verbal units, and these simple interactions are common, as when you request water and receive it or ask for directions and receive them. When we look at verbal behavior more generally and outside of therapeutic situations, the concept of discrete units like mand and tact seems far from describing most interactions between people.

Probably the most common way that verbal behavior occurs is in conversation. What, however, is a conversation? Someone taking a discrete-unit view might suggest that a conversation consists of a chain of units, each one consisting of a speaker's utterance inducing a listener's verbal response, and in which the speaker and listener exchange roles. The speaker says something, then the listener says something, but now the listener is speaker and the original speaker is now listener, and so on. Conversation, however, seems to collapse the speaker and listener roles, making the distinctions seem forced. If Tom says, "What a beautiful day!" and Jane responds, "Yes, isn't it," when exactly was Jane listener and when exactly was Jane speaker? Jane is both speaker and listener at the same time, because her verbal behavior as a response is listening, but she is speaking too.

Alternatively, conversation has been characterized as something two persons do together, in a temporary twosome, like two people singing a duet or dancing together. Studies of the development of verbal behavior in infants suggest something like this. Catherine Snow (1977) observed mothers with three-month-old infants. A mother would make sounds to the infant repeatedly, and if the infant made any kind of sound, the mother would always respond with vocalizations in return. The conversation was lopsided, but the infant's vocalizations always induced vocalization on the part of the mother. As time went on, the infant's vocalizations came to follow the mother's vocalizations more reliably. At first the infant's vocalization induced vocalization in the mother, but after a while the mother's vocalizations induced vocalization in the infant. Appearance even in infancy implies that such duets are common fare for humans from an early age.

Researchers studying development of verbal behavior have struggled to find adequate measures of progress. Age is an inaccurate reflection of physiological development, because children develop at different rates. Observations of young children often rely on "mean length of utterance" (MLU), instead of age, and MLU is taken as an index of overall competence. The unit of measurement is the *morpheme*, and MLU is the number of such functional subunits in an utterance. For example, "Where is my blankie?" has five morphemes, and "Gimme cookie" has four morphemes. Although MLU generally increases with age in normally developing children, researchers assume it to be more indicative of development than age. Using MLU, one can look for other aspects of verbal behavior that might be predicted by MLU. Figure 9.1 shows results from one study of dialogue between children ranging from under 27 months old to 61 months. The two measures shown are percentages of observations in which (1) the utterance was comprehensible to the researchers and the other child; and (2) the focus of the utterance was on the other child rather than self. Both measures increased as MLU increased.

An utterance consists of a string of sounds or signs with a pause before and after, but not only that, because the effects of an utterance depend on factors like tone, stress, and loudness ("prosody"). Consider the various ways I might say, "Please give me water." I might say, "*Please* give me some water," implying you have been recalcitrant. I might say, "Please give me some *water*," perhaps rejecting alcoholic drinks. I might hold up a glass. I might wave my hand. And so on. The same written sentence, "You are hungry" or "That is a marigold" might be a statement

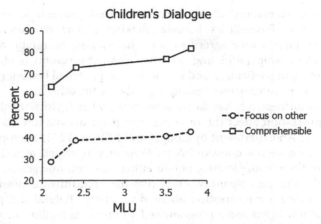

Figure 9.1 *Development of conversational competence as a function of mean length of utterance (MLU). Note*: The data were drawn from conversations between pairs out of 47 children. The solid line shows the percentage of utterances that were understood by both the experimenters and the other child. The dashed line shows the percentage of utterances that focused on the other child rather than self. Data from Naerland (2011; Table 4).

or a question, depending on prosody, which the written form fails to capture.

Tom and Jane in conversation consists of Tom-utterances inducing Jane-utterances and Jane-utterances inducing Tom-utterances. A duet like this might be thought of as an activity in which both Tom and Jane participate as a duo. We encountered this idea of multiple organisms behaving together in the last chapter when we took up the Ideal Free Distribution. In the conversation-activity, Tom's utterances and Jane's utterances are activity parts that contribute to the whole, just as the parts of a tennis serve contribute to the whole serve. If we tried to categorize the parts by their function, we might see: (1) affiliating (including agreeing and approving); (2) distancing (including disagreeing and disapproving) (3) persuading (including threatening, promising, requesting, exhorting, and cajoling); and (4) informing (including explaining and identifying). This list may prove incomplete or incorrect. Research on verbal behavior from the molar, temporally extended, viewpoint has barely begun.

A conversation, as a whole, integrated process, serves a function. Possibilities include: making a deal or purchase (each interlocutor agrees to act), maintaining or establishing a relationship (affiliating, as when the conversation is about nothing in particular), and initiating rule-governed behavior (as when one interlocutor instructs or advises the other).

Initial research has focused on time: what factors within a conversation affect the time that one party orients toward the other? An experiment by Conger and Killeen (1974) attempted to examine the question. A participant was seated at a table with three confederates, one to either side and one across the table. The participant was told that the experimenters wanted to record a conversation about drug abuse. Behind the participant, lights were programmed to go on according to two unequal VI schedules. When the light came on for the confederate to the left, that confederate waited for the first opportunity to deliver agreement such as, "Good point" or "Yes, I agree." The confederate on the right did the same when the light on the right came on. The third confederate only helped to keep the conversation going. The experimenters measured the amount of time the participant looked at the confederate on the right versus the confederate on the left. One participant was exposed to five different pairs of VI schedules. The results with that participant are shown in Figure 9.2. Although the relation is not as tight as in choice research with buttons, levers, or keys (e.g., Figure 8.2), the equation fitted to the points resembles the results from experiments with non-verbal behavior, with an exponent (slope) of 0.846 (slight undermatching).

One significant aspect of the results in Figure 9.2 is that the confederates' vocalizations were not contingent on the participant's looking toward the one vocalizing. They only had to wait for the participant to say something. Most likely, the confederates' vocalizations induced looking in the direction of the one vocalizing. In other words, the participant turned toward whoever spoke. Thus, the participant oriented longer toward whichever confederate spoke more often.

In a follow-up study, Carsta Simon experimented with the same sort of arrangement, but including conditions in which a confederate's speech occurred only on eye contact. Those

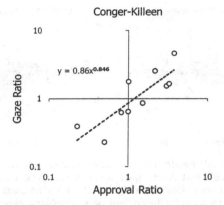

Figure 9.2 *Representative results from an experiment studying conversation and choice. Note:* The graph shows the participant's ratio of gazing at the confederate on the right to gazing at the confederate on the left as a function of the ratio of approving utterances from the confederate on the right to approving utterances from the confederate on the left. The dashed line shows how the power function fits the ratios; it appears as a line because of the logarithmic coordinates. Data from Conger and Killeen (1974).

conditions were compared with conditions, like those of Conger and Killeen, in which no eye contact was required (Simon & Baum, 2017). Simon's results differed from that earlier study and expanded the possibilities for outcomes in experiments with conversation. Simon's participants, unlike Conger's, were almost oblivious to the approval ratio. The graph on the left of Figure 9.3 shows how gaze ratio varied with approval ratio. Whether gaze was required for the confederate's approval (GR) or not required (GN), gaze ratio hardly deviated from equality (1.0) as approval ratio varied. The two lines fitted to the data points have slopes (exponents in the equations) close to zero. Simon did find a relation of gaze ratio to the confederates' speaking, but seemingly opposite to Conger's: The participants spoke and gazed at the confederate that spoke *less* often. This result is shown in the graph on the right in Figure 9.3, which shows gaze ratio as a function of the ratio of times that the confederates spent talking. The negative slopes indicate that gaze was directed more at the confederate who spoke less and less at the confederate who spoke more. The two lines for gaze

110 | Verbal Behavior and Rules

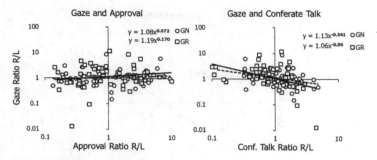

Figure 9.3 Results from the experiment by Carsta Simon on conversation and choice. Note: **Left**: Participants' gaze ratio as a function of confederates' approval ratio. The circles indicate gaze ratios from the condition in which gaze was not required for the confederates to deliver approval (GN). The squares indicate gaze ratio from the condition in which gaze was required for the confederates to deliver approval (GR). The power functions shown appear as straight lines in these logarithmic coordinates. Both exponents are close to zero, indicating that approval had almost no effect, whether gaze was required for approval or not. **Right**: Participants' gaze ratio as a function the ratio of talk duration of the confederates. Both exponents of the power functions are negative and substantially different from zero, indicating that the participants favored the confederate who spoke less over the confederate who spoke more.

required and gaze not required differ in slope (exponents in the equations), but the variability in the data makes the difference insignificant. Overall, the exponent relating gaze ratio to the ratio of confederates' speaking equaled about −0.45.

Why did Simon's results differ from Conger's? No one can say right now, but several factors might be at play. Three stand out: (1) culture; (2) maturity of the participants; and (3) gender of the participants and confederates. Any or all of these might have had effects. Simon's research was conducted in Germany with German speakers, whereas Conger's study was done in the United States with English speakers. Possibly German norms about conversation dictate that everyone should have the opportunity to speak and that approval or agreement is irrelevant. American norms, in contrast, might simply allow the participant to focus on the interlocutor that was more responsive. The difference in age of the participants in the two experiments, however, may also have been a factor. Simon's participants ranged in age from 20 to 66 years old. Conger's participants' ages ranged from 21 to 27 years. Older participants might approach conversation as a cooperative enterprise, whereas younger participants might not. The third possible factor, gender, might also have had effects. Conger's five participants included one female and four males. Simon's nine participants included five females and four males. The different ratios of females to males might have affected the results if male participants tended to orient toward a responsive interlocutor and female participants did not. Perhaps more significant, in Conger's experiment the confederates were all male, whereas in Simon's experiment the confederates were all female. Research that approaches conversation as flow and temporally extended activity has just begun and much remains to be done.

Rules

Much behavior is obviously regular. A school of fish who all move as one seems to be following rules about staying a certain distance from the others and to move in the same direction. A pigeon in an experiment on matching to sample presented with a red triangle sample pecks at the red triangle comparison rather than a green circle, and perhaps the pigeon seems to follow a rule of pecking at the matching comparison.

When behavior seems regular, however, the regularity does not mean the organism is following any rule. Rather, the rule statement serves to summarize an observer's appreciation of the regularity. The observer might say that the pigeon in the matching-to-sample experiment is responding to "same." What actually induces the pattern of behavior may differ from the observer's summary. The pigeon matching to sample, for example, may just peck at the red triangle when the sample is a red triangle, and nothing like our concept of "same" may enter in.

Following a rule depends on verbal behavior. Someone gives the rule, and someone else follows it. A parent says, "Wash your hands before you eat," and the child obeys. Giving a rule constitutes verbal behavior and is often an interaction between a speaker and a listener. To take in all examples of rules, however, we need to generalize further, because even a "no smoking" sign may be considered a rule.

A rule, then, is an inducer produced by verbal behavior, or technically, a *verbal discriminative stimulus*. Rule giving may be speech or gesture or even posting a sign. A mother exhorting her child to wash hands need not say "Wash your hands"; she might say, "What do we do now?" or make washing motions with her hands. As with other verbal behavior, a wide variety of forms giving the same rule may all be equivalent in the sense that they all induce the same activity in the one who follows the rule—hand washing in this example.

Rules usually are given for the "good" of the one following the rule, but one cannot leave out the good of the rule giver from the account of "rule-governed behavior," as rule following is often designated. The rule "Wash your hands before you eat" manifestly concerns the child's health, because washing one's hands before eating reduces the likelihood of becoming ill, and the mother has a stake in the child's remaining healthy and surviving. Somehow the mother's verbal behavior must be induced by that concern, but the covariance between hand washing and health must be extremely long and drawn out. How could it affect the mother's behavior? Something more immediate must induce her behavior. Whether in a technologically rich environment or a simpler one, someone told the mother that washing one's hands before eating is good or important. Perhaps her own parents told her, but the one giving her the rule may have been a neighbor or a doctor on the television. The rule she was given was equivalent to, "If you want your child to be healthy, make sure she washes her hands before she eats." The mother need know nothing about the germ theory of disease; she only needs to know the negative covariance between hand washing and illness.

As you may already have noticed, rules are in no sense necessarily veridical. A rule cannot be said to "describe" or "point to" a long-term relation like washing hands and good health. This is clear when rules are given in abbreviated form or as gestures. It is clear too when a stated rule contains terms that have no connection to the world of our senses, like, "You must go to church or you will burn in Hell." A rule like that aims to induce churchgoing, but the long-term relation involved has to do with the inducements of belonging to a congregation, including avoiding disapproval and gaining social and business connections, for example.

Rulemaking is verbal behavior induced by covariance itself. Someone might see covariance between telling the truth and social acceptance and say, "I have found that when I tell the truth, people are more friendly toward me. You should tell the truth too." Often rule makers are experts, like researchers who examine data and make rules like, "If you smoke, your risk of heart disease, cancer, and emphysema will increase," or "If we do not curb our emissions of greenhouse gases, we will experience more extreme and more variable weather conditions." As we noted before, the rule need not be veridical. If the actual covariance observed is covariance between going to church and social acceptance, the rule made might be about going to church and going to Hell.

Figure 9.4 diagrams the relations involved in rule-governed behavior. It follows the conventions we saw in Figure 4.1. The solid arrows indicate induction, and the dashed arrows indicate covariance. The top diagram shows the relations in general terms. At the left, a speaker's verbal behavior Bv gives the rule, an inducer that induces the listener's activity B. In the short-term relation, someone, usually the speaker, supplies further inducement (short-term PIE or proxy) upon the listener's obedience (i.e., when the rule successfully induces B). That short-term consequence would typically be approval—a vocalization, a smile, or a pat on the back—or the avoidance of disapproval. This short-term PIE, which is in covariance with both the rule and activity B (dashed arrows), also serves to induce B (solid arrow).

Like the short-term relation, the long-term relation in Figure 9.4 (top), diagrammed in accord with Figure 4.1, shows covariances between a long-term signal or context (S^D) and activity B and also a long-term PIE, like surviving and

Verbal Behavior and Rules

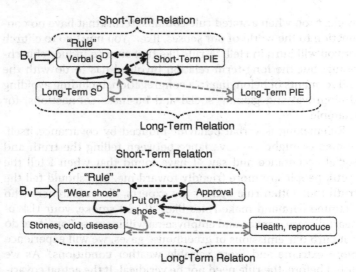

Figure 9.4 *Short-term and long-term relations inducing rule giving and rule following.* **Note**: **Top**: The relations shown in general terms. A rule giver's verbal behavior Bv produces a verbal discriminative stimulus or "rule." In the short term, the rule covaries with a short-term PIE (usually social). The short-term PIE covaries with and induces the correct activity *B* (rule following), and the rule also induces *B* because of the covariance between the rule and the short-term PIE. The long-term relations effects are colored gray because they tend to be weak. The long-term S^D covaries with the long-term PIE, and the activity *B* also covaries with the long-term PIE. If the long-term relation were effective, the long-term S^D might induce the activity. The covariance between *B* and the long-term PIE might also induce *B* (not shown; would be a solid gray arrow between long-term PIE and *B*). **Bottom**: The same relations for a specific example: putting on shoes. The rule giver's verbal behavior Bv gives something like, "You should wear shoes when you go out" or "Don't go barefoot." The rule is backed up (covaries) with approval ("Good" or "That's right") or avoidance of disapproval, and putting on shoes covaries with this inducer too. Both the rule and approval induce putting on shoes. The long-term relation may come to induce putting on shoes if one encounters untoward effects of going barefoot such as injury to the feet, which might covary with enjoying health or reproducing.

reproducing. The long-term S^D and the long-term PIE might induce activity *B*, but because the covariances are so drawn-out, these arrows are colored gray, to indicate that they may be too abstract to induce activity *B*. Sometimes the long-term relation does come to induce B directly, as when you feel better when you exercise and feeling better induces exercising, or when you see unprecedented weather and that induces talking about climate change. Often, however, the long-term relation never takes over, and the short-term relation alone induces B. Then the listener just does the "right thing." I may have no idea why honesty is good, but I may be honest because I have been told that over and over. In contrast, if the long-term relation takes over, it can induce verbal behavior in the rule follower that may induce activity B in other listeners. Whatever the rule follower says may spread activity B through the verbal community. The rule might begin with, "I have noticed that ..."

The lower diagram in Figure 9.4 diagrams an example, the rule, "If you wear shoes, you are more likely to survive and reproduce." The speaker gives the rule in some form, like saying, "You should wear shoes," or "You can't come in here barefoot," or just pointing at the listener's bare feet and wagging the finger. This verbal S^D induces putting on shoes. The short-term result is approval or removal of disapproval, and this also induces putting on shoes. Along with this short-term induction, the listener may encounter more concrete inducers like sharp stones, freezing, and hookworm. These constitute a long-term context for putting on shoes, and negative covariance between wearing shoes and injury and disease, along with the likely promotion of surviving and reproducing, also induces putting on shoes. When everyone puts on shoes, wearing shoes becomes a cultural practice and "correct" behavior. More about that in the next chapter.

Considerable research has examined the effects of rules on behavior. Many experiments compare performance when the experimenter gives a rule with performance when no rule is given. For example, participants may be exposed to a multiple schedule in which two conditions alternate, one in which presses on a button produce points according to a VR schedule when a red light is on, and one in which presses produce points according to a FI schedule when a green light is on. If the participant is given no explanation of the schedules, button-pressing may show patterns similar to the patterns seen in nonhuman animals: extremely high press rates for the VR and temporal discrimination for the FI (pausing followed by moderately high rate). If the participant is told about the schedules, these patterns emerge immediately. Sometimes, however, the experimenter gives incorrect rules, saying that high rates are correct when the light is green (FI) and low rates are correct when the light is red (VR). Illustrating a cultural norm to do as one is told by persons in authority, participants, usually undergraduates, press according to the rules given and may never shift to the schedule-typical patterns.

Another sort of experiment allows one to study all three aspects of rule governance: rule following, rule giving, and rule making. David Ruiz did an experiment like this (unpublished personal communication). Nine undergraduates participated for two sessions in a space battle game. Each session included 14 trials in random order in which two laser cannons were available for the participant to shoot at a space ship displayed in the center of the computer screen. Occasionally a shot would cause the ship to blow up with a flash of light and the sound of an explosion, and then another ship would appear. Participants were instructed to blow up as many space ships as possible. The explosions were programmed according to two VI schedules. In this context, the explosions maintained the two activities of shooting with the cannon on the left and shooting with the cannon on the right; in the parlance of Figure 4.1, the explosions were inducers. Each of the 14 trials in a session presented one of seven programmed ratios (left:right): 24:1, 8:1, 2:1, 1:1, 1:2, 1:8, and 1:24. Each trial lasted until five ships had been blown up, and a new trial began after a 15-s timeout. Toward the top of the computer screen seven circles were arranged horizontally. During seven of the trials, presenting the seven explosion ratios, all circles were lit white; this was the "no-S^D" condition. During the other seven trials, one circle was lit red, corresponding to the ratio of explosions programmed. If the ratio was 1:1, the center circle was lit red, otherwise the red circle appeared to the left or right, further according to how relatively favorable that cannon would be; this was the "S^D" condition. The data from the two sessions were pooled.

For another three participants, Ruiz followed the same procedure, with two changes: (1) all trials included the red circle ("S^D" condition); and (2) the participants were told in advance about the meaning of the red circles.

Using the amount of shooting on the left and right as the activities and the number of obtained explosions left and right as the inducers, Ruiz analyzed the preferences for the left and right cannons as the logarithms of the ratios of shots left to shots right compared to the logarithms of the ratios of explosions left to explosions right. Recalling Equation 8.3, we see how Ruiz analyzed the data:

$$log\left(\frac{B_1}{B_2}\right) = s \cdot log\left(\frac{X_1}{X_2}\right) + log b \qquad (9.1)$$

B_1 and B_2 equaled the numbers of shots from Cannon 1 and Cannon 2, X_1 and X_2 equaled the numbers of explosions obtained from shots at Cannon 1 and Cannon2, the slope S indicates sensitivity to the ratio of explosions, and $log\ b$ unequal to zero indicates some inherent bias. When S equals 1.0, the behavior ratio matches the inducer ratio. If S falls short of 1.0, which is called "undermatching," the behavior ratio is less sensitive to the inducer ratio, and when S exceeds 1.0, which is called "overmatching," the behavior ratio is hyper-sensitive to the inducer ratio. S equal to 1.0 is optimal, and undermatching and overmatching are suboptimal. Ruiz did the analysis with Equation 9.1 across explosion ratios for each successive explosion within a trial. So, he calculated behavior ratio before the first explosion, after the first and before the second, and so on, first through fifth, for each explosion ratio. With these activity ratios and explosion ratios, he fitted Equation 9.1 for each successive explosion within trials, and he analyzed the "no-S^D" and "S^D" conditions separately.

Figure 9.5 shows results from Ruiz's experiment. The graph at the upper left ("no-S^D") shows for all nine participants how sensitivity (S) started near zero (behavior ratio unaffected by explosion ratio) and gradually increased across explosions within a trial. However, sensitivity never reached 1.0, but averaged out to around 0.6, with very few points above 1.0 (matching; dashed line). The heavy line shows means across participants.

Ruiz quizzed the participants at the end of the experiment as to what strategy they used while participating, and found that

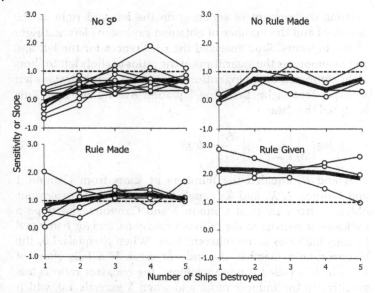

Figure 9.5 *Results from David Ruiz's experiments on rule making, rule giving, and rule following. Note:* **Upper left**: Sensitivity (S in Equation 9.1) growing across the five ships destroyed in a component in the "no-S^D" condition. The dashed line shows S equal to 1.0, matching. The thick solid line shows the mean across the nine participants. **Upper right**: Sensitivity across the five ships destroyed for the three participants in the S^D condition who made no rule. **Lower left**: Sensitivity across the five ships destroyed for the six participants in the S^D condition who made the rule. **Lower right**: Sensitivity across the five ships destroyed for three participants in the S^D condition who were given a rule.

six participants were able to explain the function of the red circle, whereas three participants were unable to state any rule. The graph at the upper right in Figure 9.5 shows the results for the three non-rule-making participants in the "S^D" condition. Their pattern of increasing sensitivity up to a level short of 1.0 resembles the pattern with no S^D in the upper left graph. For them, the red circle was irrelevant; they behaved the same in the "S^D" and the "no-S^D" conditions.

The lower left graph in Figure 9.5 shows results for the six participants that were able to state the rule about the red circle. In this "S^D" condition, two features of their results stand out: (1) five out of six began trials with sensitivity above zero (mean of 0.84); and (2) their sensitivity rose to about 1.0, which means they were approximately matching their allocation of activity time to the relative frequency of explosions, the inducers. Thus, the red circle induced more activity toward the more favorable cannon from the outset of the component and ultimately induced matching, the optimal strategy. Recalling Equations 8.1 and 8.2, we see that the matching in Figure 9.5 equates relative activity rate with relative competitive weight.

The lower right graph shows results from the three other participants in the same "S^D" procedure, but who received an explanation of the red circle at the beginning of the experiment. Their results differed from the other participants', both the ones who made no rule and the ones who made a rule. Sensitivity began and ended well above 1.0, meaning that they over-allocated time to the favorable cannon and under-allocated time to the less-favorable cannon. This is the hyper-sensitivity called "overmatching." The flatness of the lines indicates that the rule given dominated their performance from the outset of a component. Possibly, the participants who made the rule for themselves more closely approximated an optimal performance. Much remains to be understood, however, because the way the rule was given might have made a difference; they were just told that the more the red circle deviated from the center, the more favorable was the cannon indicated. Further research might clarify the exact role of a given rule in comparison with a made rule.

Rules and the practices that they induce are essential to human culture. Rule giving both transmits and spreads practices throughout a social group. Laboratory research on rule giving, rule following, and rule making may shed light on the processes involved. Much remains to be done. We will take up the phenomenon of culture, its origin, and its effects in the next chapter.

Further Reading

Conger, R., & Killeen, P. (1974). Use of concurrent operants in small group research. *Pacific Sociological Review, 17*(4), 399–416. Results for one participant appear in Figure 9.2.

Lashley, K. S. (1951). The problem of serial order in behavior. In L. A. Jeffress (Ed.), *Cerebral mechanisms in behavior* (pp. 112–136). Wiley. This paper is a classic. Lashley argues that temporally extended episodes of behavior have a wholeness to them that excludes representing them as chains of discrete units. Most of his examples are verbal utterances.

Naerland, T. (2011). Evaluating dialogue competence in naturally occurring child-child interactions. *Early Child Development and Care, 181*(5), 691–705. This study involved 47 children in four age groups. Some results appear in Figure 9.1.

Simon, C., & Baum, W. M. (2017). Allocation of speech in conversation. *Journal of the Experimental Analysis of Behavior, 107*(2), 258–278. This experiment repeated and extended the one by Conger and Killeen (1974) and produced very different results, some of which appear in Figure 9.3.

Skinner, B. F. (1957). *Verbal Behavior.* Appleton-Century-Crofts. This classic book contains Skinner's initial foray into verbal behavior, defining it and sketching some discrete units.

Snow, C. E. (1977). The development of conversation between mothers and babies. *Journal of Child Language, 4*(1), 1–22. This paper describes research with mother-baby pairs and documents interactions that serve as the basis for later development of conversation.

10

Social Behavior and Culture

In India, if you enter a home or shop owned by Hindus, you are required to remove your shoes. If you enter a home or shop owned by Zoroastrians, you are urged to keep your shoes on. Both groups, however, favor wearing shoes in the street. If you enter a Christian church, you are supposed to remove your hat. If you enter a Jewish synagogue, you are required to cover your head. Both Christians and Jews, however, would favor wearing a hat outside. Different groups have different customs or norms of behavior. We call these *cultural* differences.

What is culture? The first point to understand is that culture is a group-level phenomenon. An individual person's patterns of behavior cannot be called cultural practices unless they are shared by other people in the person's group. Cultural practices are shared by members of a group.

We may define culture as: *practices acquired as a result of membership in a group*. A *practice* is the same as what we have been calling an *activity*; all practices are activities, but not all activities are practices. To be a practice, an activity must be shared at the group level and be acquired as a result of membership in the group. Traditionally a group's culture was defined as the sum of its beliefs and values. From the perspective of a science of behavior, beliefs and values are behavior. A belief is an extended pattern of behavior, an activity. "We sacrifice to our gods" is verbal behavior and part of the practice (belief) that also includes parts like sacrificing and exhorting others to do so.

Introduction to Behavior: An Evolutionary Perspective, First Edition.
William M. Baum.
© 2024 John Wiley & Sons, Inc. Published 2024 by John Wiley & Sons, Inc.

"Thou shalt not kill" is verbal behavior indicating the value that we prefer not killing and that killing another will be punished.

Cultural practices are wide ranging. They include manufacturing and use of shelters like houses, tents, yurts, and huts, of transport like wagons, cars, and airplanes, of means of communication like telephones, televisions, computers, pens, and paper, and of weapons and tools like swords, plows, hammers, knives, guns, and sex toys. They include rites and rituals like coming-of-age ceremonies, weddings, and religious services. They include fairy tales, legends, myths, and poems—not to mention rules about keeping healthy, who should marry who, and appeasing the gods. Taken together, all these practices create both a physical environment and a social environment that both support and constrain the development of members' behavior. A person in 15th-century France would have accepted a certain position in society, as a soldier, a peasant, or an aristocrat, and behaved according to the dictates of that position. A person in 21st-century America may become a soldier, a farmer, or a politician, and behave accordingly, but with vastly different verbal behavior, not about knowing one's station, but about opportunity and success. As the rules and other practices change through time, the physical and social environments induce new and different activity patterns.

Like any activity, a practice is a whole made up of parts that are also activities but on a smaller time scale. Many of these small parts participate in more than one practice. Picking up an object and putting it in a certain place, fastening two objects together, and tying knots all might be parts of building a boat or building a shelter. Heating something over a fire might be a part of cooking or processing dyes. Most obviously, verbal practices such as rule giving, storytelling, and greeting all have shared parts—what are called "parts of speech" like words and phrases.

The key parts of the behavioral definition of culture are: (1) culture consists of practices, including verbal behavior, that occur among members of the group; and (2) that these practices are acquired and are the result of membership in the group. This latter point emphasizes ontogeny of cultural practices, rather than phylogeny.

In social groups across the animal kingdom, many are highly organized and have divisions of labor, but their organization arises more from phylogeny than ontogeny. In an ant colony, for example, the queen reproduces, the workers tend to the offspring and forage, and the soldiers protect the colony from intruders, but genes and chemicals account for the activities of the ants; they are not acquired. In some mammalian species, notably naked mole rats, which live in underground tunnels, a similar pattern occurs: only one female reproduces, and the others all serve her. The pattern is highly determined, and the activities are primarily due to phylogeny.

Culture is not necessarily uniquely human, however. Many social creatures, particularly primates, cetaceans (whales and porpoises), and corvids display traditions that clearly are based on experience with the environment and are passed along from generation to generation. Different groups of chimpanzees, for example, open the same nuts with different techniques. Crows avoid a person with a gun even if they have had no experience with guns; some previous generation did have experience with guns.

Human culture differs from other animals' cultural traditions—what we might call "proto-culture"—primarily because humans have verbal behavior. Whereas the traditions of proto-culture depend entirely on imitation, human culture relies not only on imitation but also on teaching in the form of rule governance as we saw in the preceding chapter.

Humans are a highly social species that produces complex organizations that might be compared to ant colonies, except that the organization is arrived at entirely differently. Human infants and older children grow up in an environment that shapes their activities powerfully and continuously. The children are well prepared by phylogeny to be extremely sensitive to social cues from caregivers and others around them and to be docile, to conform to the activity required of them (Simon, 1990). Cues from others readily induce correct activity in children and adults. For this function, humans are equipped with a huge array of facial expressions and bodily gestures that serve both to induce some activities and to discourage others. In a complex society like the United States, sometimes children fail to get adequate constraining guidance and end up engaging in anti-social behavior, but most children get training early and often. Recall from the previous chapter, for example, how conversation may begin even in the first few months of life.

The social cues exchanged among humans help to explain both the complexity of human cultures and their diversity. Much of the diversity of cultures is the outcome of diversity of environments that human groups find themselves in. For example, climate determines to a great extent what foods are available to exploit. Both hunting and gathering are affected. When mammoths walked the earth, hunting parties had ways to bring these enormous beasts down. Some California Indian tribes made acorns a large part of their diet, but acorns cannot be eaten without considerable processing, and the people had to develop processing techniques and pass them along from generation to generation.

Cultures are not infinitely diverse, however. The practices that evolve in a given environment are both facilitated and constrained by human physiology. For example, humans have a relatively short gut that precludes a lot of processing internal to the body. A cow has a huge gut that allows it to eat low-quality vegetation like grass; humans cannot digest raw grass. The human hand, though, affords many opportunities for hunting and processing. A carcass can be cut up with tools invented within the group, and acorns can be gathered in baskets, cooked in pots over a fire, and crushed with tools invented for the purpose.

Making boats is a common practice among groups that live near water, but the materials and methods of manufacture vary widely. Where large trees are available, a canoe may be made from a tree trunk by burning and excavating a space inside. American Indians were able to make canoes from birch bark applied to a wooden frame. Near the Arctic Circle, where no trees grow, boats are made of skins stretched on a frame.

From these observations, we see that culture serves to make a group's interactions with their environment more effective. Partly culture does this by practices that respond to environmental variation and partly by practices that exploit the environment better, as we have seen. The third way that culture improves a group's effectiveness is by modifying the environment to suit the group's surviving and reproducing. In this regard, culture may be likened to what biologists call "niche construction," the modification of the environment by parents in ways that benefit their offspring.

Earthworms offer a classic example of niche construction. As any gardener will tell you, earthworms are good for the soil. The worms constantly take in soil and secrete waste that enriches the soil, and they break up the soil to make it more friable. This improves the soil for the worms' offspring. A dramatic example of niche construction is the beaver dam. Beavers cut down small trees with their large and sharp incisor teeth. They use the trees to dam a stream and create a pond. The pond serves multiple purposes: it protects the beavers, because they can build their lodge in the middle of the pond to discourage predators; and the flooded area around the pond produces nourishing vegetation that serves as food. So, beavers' modifications of their environment promote surviving and reproducing of both the adults and their offspring.

To see how culture is like niche construction, compare the beaver dam to the many ways that humans change their environment to suit themselves. Not only do humans change the landscape by plowing soil, felling trees, and digging ditches, but they add to the environment with constructions such as igloos, mud huts, yurts, and houses. Plus, they invent tools that make manufacture of additional artifacts possible: axes, television sets, computers, airplanes, and so on.

A person growing up in the midst of a culture is shaped by both a social environment and a physical environment that together facilitate some behavioral patterns and discourage others. The social environment consists of other folks around the person giving rules and inducing compliance by punishing unwanted behavior and inducing desired behavior, rule following. Modeling correct behavior and adding rules like "we do this in our community" ensures that people wear the right garments, share food and other goods, adorn their bodies with tattoos and scars, greet others properly, speak the right language or dialect, and so on. The rules and inducements for correct behavior characterize a culture, define its uniqueness, and mark the members of the group distinctly.

In the 19th and 20th centuries, anthropologists accumulated a tremendous amount of data on cultures all over the world. Researchers interested in culture today draw on the body of descriptive data and take the study further by examining the way that groups adapt to their environment. For example, questions arise as to how groups managed to feed themselves while still keeping their population stable. How did they extract all needed nutrients from their environment? Or natural experiments occur, as for example, the rise of open-source software presenting an example of many individuals cooperating with others to achieve working results.

Experiments

Experiments aiming to shed light on cultural processes focus primarily on two phenomena: (a) the extraordinary level of cooperation among humans, even strangers; and (b) the way culture produces cumulative effects—that is, practices that grow in complexity and effectiveness over time and across generations. Inquiries into the bases of human cooperation often use *games*. A game is an interaction between two or more people in which the actions of each affect the outcomes of others. Many different games have been studied. Common ones are: the dictator game; the ultimatum game; and social-dilemma games. In the *dictator* game, you are given an amount of money (e.g., $10) and asked how much of it you would like to give to someone else, usually a member of your community, but an anonymous stranger. People in different cultures respond differently, in small-scale societies tending to give little and in industrialized societies about half (Henrich et al., 2006). The norms of sharing vary widely.

In the *ultimatum* game, you are given the same amount of money and asked how much you want to give to the other, but this time the other person can refuse the amount offered, with the result that neither person gets any money. Thus, the recipient has the option to punish a violation of the sharing norm. In this game, again the outcome in Western industrialized societies tends to equal sharing, but again results vary across cultures; small-scale groups often allow unequal distribution. Some groups actually refuse offers of more than half (Henrich et al., 2006).

The most-studied social-dilemma games are the *prisoners' dilemma* and the *public-goods* game. The prisoners' dilemma derives from a scenario in which two suspects are detained by the police and held in separate rooms. Each suspect has the option of remaining silent—that is, cooperating with the other—or confessing, throwing the blame on the other—called "defecting." So, they may both cooperate, they may both defect, or one may cooperate and the other defect. Figure 10.1A shows the outcomes for the different combinations that make the game a dilemma. Their best strategy is to both cooperate, because they only serve a year in prison, but each might be tempted to defect, because the defector does no jail time. If they both defect, however, the outcome is bad, because they serve three years. Figure 10.1B shows a positive version of the same

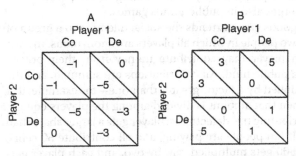

Figure 10.1 *Actions and payoffs in Prisoners' Dilemma games. Note*: The two players have the options to cooperate with one another (Co) or defect and betray one another (De). If both cooperate, they pay a small price or gain a bit less. If one defects while the other cooperates, the defector makes out well, but the cooperator has the worst outcome. If both defect, the outcome is bad for both. The dilemma arises from the temptation to defect. **A**: a game in which the outcomes are zero or negative (e.g., years in prison). **B**: a game in which the outcomes are zero or positive (e.g., money or praise).

dilemma. For example, suppose the players work together on a project. If both cooperate, they earn three points each, but the temptation exists for one to take all the proceeds (five points; defect) and leave the other nothing. If both defect, they wind up with a poor product or little credit (one point). As with the dictator game and the ultimatum game, the degree of cooperation varies across cultures and also according to other factors like whether the players talk to one another before the game, which increases the tendency to cooperate.

When the prisoners' dilemma runs for multiple rounds, questions about strategy may arise. Suppose, for example, the game in Figure 10.1B runs for ten rounds. If both players cooperate, they will each earn 30 points. If one player defects, how should the other player respond? The question itself assumes that players are trying to maximize winnings. If one player defects in the first round, the second player may defect in the second round, but such a tit-for-tat strategy turns out not to be the best, because both players may end up defecting for the next eight rounds and lose out. Instead, the best strategy is to tolerate some defection, continuing to cooperate for a round or two to convince the other player that you are willing to cooperate. This strategy emerges also in public-goods games.

A public-goods game extends the social dilemma to a group of more than two people in which all players are anonymous. In each round, each player may contribute money from their private account to a public fund. All contributions are summed, and the sum is multiplied by a factor greater than one—for example, it is doubled. Then that amount is divided among the players equally. By not contributing (i.e. defecting) a player gets a larger share than the others. If ten people are playing, and all contribute 50 cents, the sum of 500 gets multiplied, say, by two, and each player gets back 100 cents, making a profit of 50 cents. If nine players contribute 50 cents and one player contributes nothing, the defector earns 90 cents, while all the others earn a net of only 40 cents (90 minus 50). However, if nobody contributes anything, nobody earns anything. How should the group deal with this dilemma?

The group can do nothing about defection unless they are given some tools to deal with it. Perhaps the simplest tool is anonymous communication. Figure 10.2 shows the results of an experiment with groups of five people in which players could write messages that were read aloud to the group. One series of games included no messaging, and the other series included messaging. Mean contribution in cents is shown as a function of each round of the 10-round games. The messaging, which consisted largely of urging everyone to contribute, increased the mean contribution, even though the messages were anonymous and could not be backed up with sanctions.

In some variations of public-goods games, the players are given the ability to sanction other players. This is typically done by allowing players to punish other players by imposing fines. For example, at the end of each round, each player can single out other players' contributions and impose a fine, or each player can make a rule that anyone who contributes less than a certain

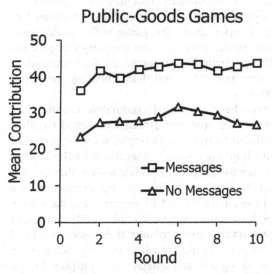

Figure 10.2 *Results from a Public-Goods game in which participants could or could not send messages to the other participants.* Note: Contributions were higher when messages were allowed, even though participants were anonymous and could not back up the messages with sanctions. Data from Baum et al. (2012).

amount is fined. Across cultures, most people in these games punish those who contribute too little ("free riders"), but, in a few cultures some people actually punished those who contributed generously (Henrich et al., 2006). Perhaps in an authoritarian state, people who cooperate may be viewed with suspicion as being government agents.

In one experiment, participants were given experience with two different public-goods games, one game including the option to punish free-riding and one without punishment. They played for 30 rounds. On each round, a participant made three decisions: (a) whether to play the game with punishment or the one without punishment; (b) contribute to the public fund and see the outcome of the round; and (c) if, having chosen the game with punishment, whether to punish any free riders. In the early rounds, most participants chose to play the punishment-free game, but more and more chose the game with punishment as rounds went on, until by the end over 90 percent of the participants were choosing the game with punishment of free-riding. When people chose the game with punishment, they tended to contribute more, and the frequency of punishing decreased. The participants preferred an environment in which cheating was punished and less cheating occurred (Gürerk et al., 2006).

Fewer experiments have examined cumulative culture than cooperation, probably because experiments designed to allow cumulating are difficult to run. For example, suppose you want to see if an artifact improves across generations in the laboratory. You have to give the players materials with which to construct, say, a basket. They construct an approximation to a basket, but how to evaluate it? In this experiment, the basket was loaded to see how much weight it could hold. In another experiment, players made paper airplanes; these were evaluated by the distance the plane could fly when thrown. But how to evaluate computer-designed arrowheads or complex knots? These evaluations may be inaccurate, but an even bigger problem concerns how to pass expertise from one generation to another. Who and how many should model the achievement of a group for the next group to take up the task?

In one well-conducted experiment, groups of three worked separately on solving a large jigsaw puzzle (Kempe & Mesoudi, 2014). They always started from scratch and were given 12 minutes to solve as much as possible. The next group got to see what the group before had done. The experiment went through four generations. The number of pieces completed increased across the four generations.

Another approach to understanding the processes of cumulative culture focuses on behavior itself increasing in effectiveness across generations when groups are challenged to respond to a situation that requires complex choices under uncertainty. For example, in one experiment groups of four people earned money by solving anagrams (Baum et al., 2004). They chose between anagrams printed on blue cards and printed on red cards for 12 minutes a generation and tried to solve as many as possible. If they solved a red anagram they each received ten cents and were offered another anagram to solve. If they solved a blue anagram they each received 25 cents but then had a timeout during which they could solve no anagrams. They chose by consensus. Assuming that they want to make as much money as possible, should they choose red or blue? Only enough experience could decide, because they were not told the duration of the timeout, and variation in the time to solve an anagram made judging which produced money at a higher rate difficult. At the end of 12 minutes, one member of the group who had been in the experiment longest was replaced with an inexperienced new member. The others immediately began instructing the newcomer as to their strategy, giving rules like, "We choose red" or "We choose blue" and urging the newcomer to go along, sometimes even misrepresenting the timeout duration. The timeout duration after solving a blue anagram varied across three conditions: one minute, when blue would be the better choice, two minutes, when neither was favored, or three minutes, when red would be the better choice.

Figure 10.3 shows some results from this experiment. The three lines show means across six replications of at least 11 generations each. Each line shows the gradual evolution of a tradition of choosing across generations. None of them finally ends

Social Behavior and Culture

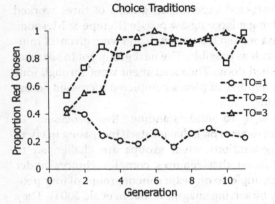

Figure 10.3 *Cumulative cultural traditions of choosing in decision-making under uncertainty. Note*: Groups of four participants chose either red or blue anagrams to solve when rate of earnings was uncertain. Each generation lasted 12 minutes, and then one member was replaced with a naïve newcomer. Choosing blue resulted in 25 cents but then required a timeout from solving anagrams. Choosing red resulted in 10 cents and allowed moving immediately on to another anagram. When the timeout was long (three minutes), more money could be earned by choosing red, and a tradition of choosing red evolved. When the timeout was short (one minute), more money could be earned by choosing blue, and a tradition of choosing blue evolved. An intermediate timeout (two minutes) favored neither color, but a tradition of choosing red evolved anyway, revealing bias for continuing the task. Data from Baum et al. (2004).

with 100 percent choice of red or blue, primarily because when all four participants had never experienced one option they often chose the non-preferred option just to see what it was. When covariance between choosing red and rate of earning money was positive or near zero, choosing red—the option that allowed immediate resumption of the task—became the tradition. When covariance between choosing red and rate of earning was negative, choosing blue, the option that entailed a one-minute timeout, became the tradition. Evolution of these traditions across generations suggests that the experiment produced a model of cumulative culture in the laboratory.

An experimental design that combines evolution of cooperation with cumulative culture exists also. The procedure requires each group to play a public-goods game for ten rounds and then leave advice for the next group that plays the same game. Each group constitutes a generation, but, unrealistically, that entire generation is replaced. This procedure offers the advantage that it is logistically easier to run than a procedure like the anagrams experiment, replacing individual players. Across six generations, Chaudhuri and his students found evolution of contributions in a public-goods game (Chaudhuri et al., 2006).

Whereas studies of the history and evolution of existing cultures afford insight into the outcomes and effects of cultural evolution, experiments with groups (called "microsocieties") in the laboratory hold the promise of shedding light on how cultural evolution works—that is, the processes by which a society's practices change over time and drive diversity across cultures. The examples we have seen here show the sort of experiments that have been done. Much scope remains for more experiments that might shed further light.

Further Reading

Baum, W. M., Paciotti, B., Richerson, P., Lubell, M., & McElreath, R. (2012). Cooperation due to cultural norms, not individual reputation. *Behavioural Processes, 91*(1), 90–93. In a public-goods game, anonymous messages increased contributions. Some data from this experiment appear in Figure 10.2.

Baum, W. M., Richerson, P. J., Efferson, C. M., & Paciotti, B. M. (2004). Cultural evolution in laboratory microsocieties including traditions of rule giving and rule following. *Evolution and Human Behavior, 25*(5), 305–326. In this experiment, groups solved anagrams cooperatively, and every generation a new person replaced someone in the group. Some data from this study appear in Figure 10.3.

Chaudhuri, A., Graziano, S., & Maitra, P. (2006). Social learning and norms in a public goods experiment with inter-generational advice. *Review of Economic Studies, 73*(2), 357–380. One of the first studies of cultural evolution in the laboratory. Transmission from earlier to later groups occurred via written advice.

Gürerk, Ö., Irlenbusch, B., & Rockenbach, B. (2006). The competitive advantage of sanctioning institutions. *Science, 312*(5770), 108–111. This experiment compared two public-goods games, one with punishment for free-riders and one without, by allowing participants to choose which to play. Over 90 percent of participants eventually preferred the game in which players could punish free-riders.

Henrich, J., McElreath, R., Barr, A., Ensminger, J., Barrett, C., Bolyanatz, A., Cardenas, J. C., Gurven, M., Gwako, E., Henrich, N., Lesorogol, C., Marlowe, F., Tracer, D., & Ziker, J. (2006). Costly punishment across human societies. *Science, 312*(5781), 1767–1770. This study compared people from 15 different cultures as to which outcomes in ultimatum games and public-goods games they would accept and which outcomes they would punish.

Kempe, M., & Mesoudi, A. (2014). An experimental demonstration of the effect of group size on cultural accumulation. *Evolution and Human Behavior, 35*(4), 285–290. Groups of people solved a jigsaw puzzle for a limited time. When they were allowed to see what the group before them had done, amount of the puzzle solved increased across generations.

Simon, H. A. (1990). A mechanism for social selection and successful altruism. *Science, 250*(4988), 1665–1668. This paper describes the concept of docility and argues that it is the product of natural selection.

11

Coda for Instructors

Anyone familiar with behavior analysis of the 20th century will have noticed the conspicuous absence of the words "reinforcer" and "reinforcement" from this book. The only place where "reinforcement" appears is in Chapter 4, where the traditional names for the covariances supporting operant behavior are given. Instead, I have relied on the concepts of *phylogenetically important event* (PIE) and *induction* to give an account of behavior, both operant and non-operant, in the light of evolutionary theory.

Several reasons lay behind those choices. First of all, nothing about living organisms can be understood today without evolutionary theory. Why do events called "reinforcers" and "punishers" affect behavior? That question cannot be adequately answered without evolutionary theory, because those events are obviously related to fitness or reproductive success. For many millions of years, organisms had to deal with prey, mates, predators, and disease, and they dealt with them both physiologically and behaviorally. Those individuals that dealt with PIEs more successfully left more offspring and hence are represented in today's populations. Borgstede and Eggert (2021) made the formal connection between reinforcement and natural selection explicit. In so doing they called phylogenetically important events "statistical fitness predictors," a label that reflects their project.

Introduction to Behavior: An Evolutionary Perspective, First Edition.
William M. Baum.
© 2024 John Wiley & Sons, Inc. Published 2024 by John Wiley & Sons, Inc.

The concepts of reinforcement, punishment, and operant behavior stem from the perception that consequences affect behavior. Fundamental questions arise: What makes an event a "consequence?" Just following action, or is some form of covariance required? How do "consequences" affect behavior? Are hypothetical constructs like "strength" required? I have aimed to answer these questions by relying on covariance and induction, concepts that have broad explanatory power without invoking hypothetical constructs.

The main reason that I have moved away from reinforcement theory is its inadequacy. One consideration we can put aside immediately is the inadequacy of temporal contiguity as a principle for explaining behavior. Psychology inherited it from 19th-century associationism and Pavlov, but even if it served for a time, contiguity-based theory never became plausible, for at least two reasons: (a) it required discrete events, whereas the world is full of continuous activities and continuous products; and (b) behavior is often influenced by events not at all contiguous with it. More than this, however, when we see how consequences maintain behavior, only viewing relations as temporally extended—at least relations between rates of events—makes any sense.

What exactly does "reinforcement" explain? The theory depends on the core idea that discrete responses are "strengthened" when followed by reinforcers. This begs questions: What is the ontological status of "strength"? And how could strength cause responses? If we think that these questions have sensible answers, still the explanatory power of "reinforcement" is weak and limited. About all it might explain is why positive reinforcement works.

Skinner (1950) claimed that the Law of Effect is no theory, it is a fact. The statement is not exactly correct. True, as Skinner pointed out, if you put a hungry rat into a chamber with a lever that, when operated delivers food, the rat will come to operate the lever. But the Law of Effect was a *theory* that was supposed to explain *that* fact. Skinner (1948) claimed that whenever food was presented it must strengthen whatever behavior immediately preceded it. That theory is false or at least extremely limited in application. His own data contradicted it (Baum, 2012).

I have relied on the concept of induction in this book because induction has much greater explanatory breadth and plausibility than reinforcement. Let us count the ways. First, induction explains both adjunctive behavior and positive reinforcement. It explains adjunctive behavior because a PIE induces activities that are related to it, either phylogenetically or ontogenetically. If an activity is in covariance with a PIE, that (operant) activity is induced by the PIE and its proxies—that is so-called positive reinforcement. Notably, activities that are induced because they covary with a PIE are specific to the PIE—whether food inducing procurement or electric shock inducing avoidance, for example. A concept like "arousal" falls short because it connotes a nonspecific effect on behavior and, unless carefully defined as a process, implies a hypothetical construct. Induction also takes account of biases as to which activities can go with which PIEs ("reinforcers"), often pointed out in the 1970s to show the limitations of reinforcement theory. The specificity of activities induced by PIEs accounts for such biases.

Second, induction solves the problem of the *first instance*—the need for an activity to occur before it can be "reinforced." Reinforcement theory has no solution for this problem; it has to appeal to some other process. For induction, the "problem" never arises. As diagrammed in Figures 4.1 and 6.1, the PIE induces activities that then may be made to covary with the PIE. When an activity covaries with the PIE that induces it, the (operant) activity is maintained.

Third, induction supplies a mechanism for stimulus control. When students are taught about "reinforcement," they are told that it always occurs in a context or the presence of a discriminative stimulus. Skinner taught that the stimulus "sets the occasion" for reinforcement. That statement, however, is just a description of what happens when a discrimination is trained. If a pigeon pecks at a green light and not at a red, what is it about the green light that results in pecking? Reinforcement theory is silent about this, although one might guess that a remnant of associationism lurks behind the portrait. In contrast, induction specifies the mechanism that underlies the discrimination: the green light induces pecking because the green light covaries with food and the red one does not.

Fourth, induction provides a straightforward account of avoidance. Reinforcement theory never offered a plausible account. The problem is that following a successful avoidance response, *nothing happens*; that is the point of avoidance. So-called two-factor theory was an attempt to somehow rescue this obvious failure of reinforcement with a fairy tale. Supposedly the context elicited an unseen "fear," and the avoidance activity either reduced this "fear" or offered "safety." Such appeals to unseen hidden constructs cannot stand scientific scrutiny. In contrast, induction offers a sound account of avoidance as soon as one escapes from the burden of requiring contiguous consequences for the avoidance activity. The explanation points to two features of avoidance: (a) avoidance activity is in negative covariance with the PIE (electric shock in experiments); and (b) avoidance never reduces the rate of the PIE to zero. The received shocks induce the avoidance activity according to a power function (Figure 4.3 here; see Baum, 2020). In other words, avoidance is maintained by its failures. When avoidance becomes lax, the event to be avoided occurs and induces the activity again.

Fifth, induction solves a basic problem in behavior analysis: the activity rates maintained by interval schedules. Reinforcement theory offered only an explanation of why interval schedules maintain rates lower than ratio schedules, but not why ratio schedules maintain such high rates or why interval schedules maintain moderately high rates too. Differential reinforcement of inter-response times meant that rates on a variable-interval (VI) schedule would be lower but also made the false prediction that rates should be extremely low—low enough that every response would produce food. One might argue that ratio schedules maintain high rates because reinforcer rate varies directly with response rate, but that relation could just as well predict zero rates as maximal rates. Induction, however, can explain: (a) the high rates on ratio schedules; (b) the tendency to quit when the ratio is too large ("ratio strain"); and (c) the intermediate activity rates maintained by VI schedules. The sketch of an explanation appears in Chapter 6, illustrated by Figures 6.2, 6.3, and 6.4. It relies on disequilibrium between activity rate and food rate, a disequilibrium that never ceases on a ratio schedule and that does cease at a moderately high activity rate on a VI schedule.

I doubt that this list is exhaustive, but it might suffice to open one up to considering the inadequacy of reinforcement in comparison with induction. Older behavior analysts used to thinking in terms of reinforcement may have difficulty changing to thinking in terms of induction. Younger scientists interested in behavior might be more open to change.

Further Reading

Baum, W. M. (2012). Rethinking reinforcement: Allocation, induction, and contingency. *Journal of the Experimental Analysis of Behavior, 97,* 101–124. https://doi.org/10.1901/jeab.2012.97-101

Baum, W. M. (2020). Avoidance, induction, and the illusion of reinforcement. *Journal of the Experimental Analysis of Behavior, 114,* 116–141. https://doi.org/10.1002/jeab.615

Borgstede, M., & Eggert, F. (2021). The formal foundation of an evolutionary theory of reinforcement. *Behavioural Processes, 186,* 1–9. https://doi.org/10.1016/j.beproc.2021.104370

Skinner, B. F. (1948). "Superstition" in the pigeon. *Journal of Experimental Psychology, 38,* 168–172. https://doi.org/10.1037/h0055873

Skinner, B. F. (1950). Are theories of learning necessary? *Psychological Review, 57,* 193–216. https://doi.org/10.1037/h0054367

Index

Note: page numbers in *italics* refer to figures; those in **bold** to tables.

a
acquisition, 56–58
  by induction, 56–58
  speed of, 57–58
activities, 11–18, *12*
  acquisition, 56–58
  cessation of old, 56
  competitive weight, 87–88, 91–94
  composed of parts, *14*, 14–15
  differential reinforcement of alternate, 40
  episodic, measurement of, 46, *47*, 48, 50
  extended, 37
  function of, 43–45
  impulsive, 39–40
  induction of, 22–23
  introduction of new, 56
  operant, 33, 64–65, 103–104, 136–137
  practice, 121–123
  process-parts, 11–12, 16
  species-specific, 24
  time allocation, 14, *14*
  time scales, *15*, 15–16
  variability, 46
activity-effect relation, 58–60
activity-part, 85–86, 107
activity rate, *34*, 34–35, 58, *61–62*, 61–66, *64–65*, 68, 69, 138–139
adaptation
  evolution, 55
  of groups to environment, 126
addiction, 97
adjunctive behavior, 137
aggregation, *47*, 48
aggression, 23, 50–51, *50–51*
ambush predation, 19
amoeba, 1, 2, 4–5, 22, 27
amount ratio, 92, 94
anagram, 131–133, *132*
ants, 123

Introduction to Behavior: An Evolutionary Perspective, First Edition.
William M. Baum.
© 2024 John Wiley & Sons, Inc. Published 2024 by John Wiley & Sons, Inc.

arousal, 22, 137
associationism, 136–137
autoshaping, 28, 57
aversion, 31, 35, 74
aversive stimuli, 23
avoidance, 23, 38, 40, 44–45, 137–138
  discrimination, 70
  poison, 35
  risk, 19–20

b

bacteria, 1, 5–7, *6*, 9–10
balance, 85–86
beavers, 10, 125
behavior, 9–20
behavior-environment feedback system, 35, *62*, 62–63
behavior-PIE relations, types of, *37*, 37–40
belief, 121
Bell, Ken, 99
bioluminescent bacteria, *6*, 6–7
boats, construction of, 124
Bobcat, 56
body language, 104
Borgstede, M., 135
Bower Bird, 44
Burmese python, 56

c

categories, 76–77
cells, 4–7, *7*
change, 3, 7, 55–56
Chaudhuri, A., 133
choice, 88–97
  concurrent VI schedules in pigeons, *90*
  conversation and, *109–110*

immediacy, effects of, 92–94, *93*
  in relation to relative amount, 91–92, *92*
  self-control, 95–97
  short-term *versus* long-term, 95–97, *96*
  in vigilance task, *91*
communities, 13
comparisons, 78–80, **79**
competition, 10, 86
competitive weight, *87*, 87–88, 91–95
concepts, 74–75, 77
concurrent schedule, 82
conditional inducer, 28, 32–33, 36
conditional reflex, 26
conditional response, 26
conditional stimulus, 25, 26, 28
conditioning, 25, 26
Conger, R., 108–111, *109*
connections, 13
consequences, 136
contiguity-based theory, 136
conversation, 105–111, *107*, *109–110*, 124
cooperation, 126–128, *127*, 130, 133
correct behavior, rules and inducements for, 125–126
correlation, 31–32, 45
courtship, 16–17
covariance, 31–40, 136
  negative, 29, *29*, *34*, 34–35, *36–37*, 37–39, 112, 138
  PIE and, *29*, 29–30, 32–40, *33–34*, *36–37*, *57*, 57–58, 74, 76, 81, 137–138

positive, 29, *29*, 33, *33*, 34, *34*, 36–39, *37*, 60
rules and, 112–113
speed of acquisition, 57–58
tightness, 88
types of behavior-PIE relations, *37*, 37–40
criminal activity, relative competitive weight of, 94–95
cues, 123–124
cultural differences, 121
cultural practices, 121–122, 124–126, 133
culture, 10, 121–133
   cumulative, 130–133, *132*
   definitions, 121–122
   in social creatures, 123
cycles, 7

d

death, 2–3, 6
delay, 92–95
deselection
   negative, *37*, 39–40
   positive, *37*, 38–40
dictator game, 126
discounting function, *96*, 96–97
discrimination, 73–77, *77*, 80–82, 137–138
   between categories, 76
   extinction as, 70
   relational, 76–77, *77*
   simultaneous, 82
   of smells, 73
   successive, 81
   temporal, 26, 66–67, 115
   trained in Pavlov's experiments, 26, 28
   training equivalences, 76

discriminative stimulus, 76, 80–81, 112, *114*, 137
diseases, 10
distance, 18
diversity, 124
DNA, 5, 7, 9–10
dogs
   in Pavlov's experiments, 24–28, *25*, 30
   smell discrimination, 73
duration, variability in, 46
dysfunctional behavior, 44, 95

e

earthworm, 125
Eggert, F., 135
electric shock, 23, 40, 44, 70, 137–138
elicitation, 22
entropy, 2–3, 6
environment
   behavior-environment feedback system, 35, *62*, 62–63
   niche construction, 125
   social behavior and culture, 122–126, 130
episodic activities, measurement of, 46, *47*, 48, 50
equilibrium, 2
equivalence, 75–80, **79**
   verbal behavior, 103–104
error, 17, 20
ethologists, 24
evolution
   adaptation, 55
   of cooperation with cumulative culture, 133
   of traditions, 132

exchange, 2–3
extinction, 56, 67, 67–70, 81–82
eye contact, 108–109

f
feedback, 17–20, *18*
  behavior-environment system, 35, *62*, 62–63
  negative, 19–20
  positive, 20
feedback function, 35
  interval schedules, 58, *59*
  ratio schedules, *61*, 61–62
fidelity, 10
first instance, 137
fixed action patterns, 24
fixed interval (FI) schedule, 60, 66, 115–116
fixed ratio (FR) schedule, 60–62, 81–82
food aversions, 74
foraging, group, 97–101
free riders, 130
function, 43–45
functional analysis, 44–45, *45*

g
gaining resources, 46, *47*, 48–49
games, 126–133
gaze ratio, *109*, 109–110
gestures, 112
group foraging, 97–101
group selection, 10

h
Hawaiian Bobtail Squid, *6*, 6–7, 28
hyper-sensitivity, 117, 119

i
Ideal Free Distribution, *98*, 98–100, *100*
imitation, 57, 123
immediacy, 92–94, *93*
  self-control, 95–97
impulsive activities, 39–40
indifference point, *96*, 96–97
inducers, 22, 44–45, 73–74, 76, 86–89, 91–94
  amount/magnitude of, 88, 94
  conditional, 28, 32–33, 36
  equivalent, 76
  extinction when lack of, 67
  immediacy of, 88, 94
  rate of, 87–88, 94
  rules, 112, 116–117, 119
  social, 94
induction, 17, 22–23, 27–29, 32–33, *33*, 35–38, 135–139
  acquisition, 56–58
  of concepts, 74–75
  level, factors influencing, 87–88
  as process, 22
  rule-governed behavior, 113
  time allocation, 86, *87*
  verbal behavior, 104, 113, 115
infections, 10
instinctive behavior, 103
instrumental activity, 33
interact, 11, 17
interactor, 10, 11
interval schedules, 60–70, 138–139
irrational activities, 27–28

j
Jennings, H. S., 1

k
Killeen, P., 108–109, *109*
Kraft, John, 99, 101

l
language, 104
Law of Allocation, *87*
Law of Effect, 136–137
learning set, 80
lek, 32, 36
listener, 103–105, 112–113, 115
living, 104

m
mand, 104–105
matching, 87, 89–92, 97, 99, 101, 117, 119
matching to sample, 78–80, *79*, 111
mean length of utterance (MLU), 106, *107*
measurement, 43–52
mechanism, 22
mental rotation, 78, *78*, 82
microbiome, 5–6
micro-organisms, 5
microsocieties, 133
MLU (mean length of utterance), 106, *107*
modeling, 125
money, temporal discounting of, *96*, 96–97
monkey, 76–77, 80
morpheme, 106

multicellular organisms, 5
multiple schedules, 81, 115–116

n
naked mole rats, 123
natural selection, 16, 22
  reinforcement connection with, 135
  sexual selection capped by, 20
negative covariance, 29, *29*, *34*, 34–35, *36–37*, 37–39, 112, 138
negative deselection, *37*, 39–40
negative punishment, *37*, 39
negative reinforcement, *37*, 38
negative selection, *37*, 38
niche construction, 125
non-verbal behavior, 108

o
ontogeny, 17, 35, 122–123
operant activity, 33, 64–65, 103–104, 136–137
organism, 1–7, 9–12, 16–17, *18*
organism-process, 9, 11
organs, 4, 5
overmatching, 117, 119

p
parts, 3–4, 85–86
  activities as composed of, *14*, 14–15
  of a practice, 122
Pavlov, Ivan Petrovich, 24–28, *25*, 30, 68, 73, 136
person/no person experiment, 81–82

phenotypic plasticity, 55
phylogenetically important
    event (PIE), 22–23, 27–30,
    29, 135
  acquisition by induction,
      57–58
  covariance and, 29, 29–30,
      32–40, 33–34, 36–37, 57,
      57–58, 74, 76, 81, 137–138
  interval schedules, 63, 64, 66
  ratio schedules, 61, 61
  rule-governed behavior, 113,
      114
  types of behavior-PIE
      relations, 37, 37–40
phylogeny, 16, 22, 36, 122–123
PIE. see phylogenetically
    important event
pigeons, 21–23, 26–28, 30,
    50–51, 50–52, 57, 61,
    63–68, 64, 67, 70, 73–78,
    81–82, 89, 98, 99, 111
poison avoidance, 35
polydipsia, 23
population, 10–11, 16
positive covariance, 29, 29, 33,
    33, 34, 34, 36–39, 37, 60
positive deselection, 37, 38–40
positive punishment, 37, 38
positive reinforcement, 37,
    38–39, 137
positive selection, 37, 38–40
practice, 121–122, 124–126,
    133
predation, ambush, 19
prisoner's dilemma game, 127,
    127–128
problem behavior, functional
    analysis of, 44–45, 45

process, 3–7
  cultural, 126
  feedback effects, 25
  induction as, 22
process-parts, 11–12, 16. see
    also activities
prosody, 106–107
proto-culture, 123
psychic secretion, 24–25, 28
public-goods game, 128–130,
    129, 133
punishers, 135
punishment, 37, 38, 40, 136
  interval schedules, 60
  negative, 37, 39
  positive, 37, 38
  public-goods game, 130
  ratio schedules, 60

r
rate ratio, 89, 92, 94
ratio schedules, 60–62, 61, 64,
    138–139
ratio strain, 138
rats, 23, 27–28, 30, 44, 51–52,
    52, 57–58, 60, 65, 65–66,
    69, 73–74, 103–104, 136
reflex, 25–26
Reid, R. L., 68
reinforcement, 135–139
  differential of alternate
      activities, 40
  negative, 37, 38
  positive, 37, 38–39
reinforcer, 135–137
reinstatement, 67–68, 68
relational discrimination,
    76–77, 77
releasers, 24, 27

replication of DNA, 9–10
replicator, 10
reproducing, 10–13, *12*, 16,
  19–20, 43–44, 49
response, to stimulus, 25–27
resurgence, 69, *69*
Ruiz, David, 116–117, *118*
rule-governed behavior,
  112–113
rules, 111–119, *114*, *118*
  culture and, 122–123,
  125–126, 129, 131

s

salivation, in Pavlov's
  experiments, 24–28, *25*, 30
searching, 17–18, 85–86
second law of thermodynamics,
  2–3
selection
  group, 10
  negative, *37*, 38
  positive, *37*, 38–40
  sexual, *12*, 13–14, 20
self-control, 95–97
sexual selection, *12*, 13–14, 20
signal, 26–30, *29*, 32–33, *33*, *36*
Simon, Carsta, 108–111
simultaneous discrimination,
  82
skills, 56
Skinner, B. F., 104, 136–137
slime molds, 4–5
smell, 73
Snow, Catherine, 105
social behavior, 121–133
social capital, 13
social cues, 123–124
social dilemma game, 126–128
social inducers, 94
speaker, 103–105, 110,
  112–113, 115
spontaneous recovery, 68
spores, 4–5
stability, 56
statistical fitness predictors,
  135
Stickleback, 24, 27, 74
stimulus, 25–30, *26*, 33, 35,
  73–82
  aversive, 23
  categories, 76–77
  discriminative, 76, 80–81
  response to, 25–27
  verbal discriminative, 112,
  114
strength, 136
strict matching, 89, 91
successive discrimination, 81
surviving, 10–13, *12*, 19–20,
  43–44
symbiosis, 5–6

t

tact, 104–105
task completion, 18–19
taste aversion, 31, 35
temporal discounting of money,
  96, 96–97
temporal discrimination, 26,
  66–67, 115
thermodynamics, 2–3
time allocation, 14, *14*, *48–50*,
  48–52, 86, *87*
timeframes
  conflict of, 95
  task completion, 18
time penalty, 92

Index

time scales, *15*, 15–16, 19, 85–86, 122
timing, 85
traditions, 123, 131–132, *132*
training discrimination, 76–78, **79**, 80
two-factor theory, 138

U
ultimatum game, 126–127
unconditional reflex, 26
unconditional response, 26
unconditional stimulus, *25*, 26
undermatching, 89–92, 99, 117
utterance, 106–107, *107*

V
values, 121
variability, 46
variable interval (VI) schedule, *59*, 60, 63–67, *64–65*, 81–82, 89, *90*, 91–93, 108, 138–139
variable ratio (VR) schedule, *59*, 60–64
variable time (VT) schedule, *65*, 66
verbal behavior, 103–111, *107*, *109–110*, 121–123
rules, 111–119, *114*
verbal community, 103–104, 115
verbal discriminative stimulus, 112, *114*
verbal units, 104–105
vigilance, 85–86, *91*
visual cue, 103
VR schedule, 115–116

W
waiting, 18–19, 58–60
working, 58–59